TRANSFER PRICING AND PERFORMANCE EVALUATION IN MULTINATIONAL CORPORATIONS

A Survey Study

Penelope J. Yunker

PRAEGER

PRAEGER SPECIAL STUDIES • PRAEGER SCIENTIFIC

Library of Congress Cataloging in Publication Data

Yunker, Penelope J.
   Transfer pricing and performance evaluation
in multinational corporations.

   Bibliography: p.
   Includes index.
   1. International business enterprises--
Management.   2. Executives--Rating of.
3. Transfer pricing.   I. Title.
HD62.4.Y86   1982   658'.049   82-13201
ISBN 0-03-062047-3

$$HD$$
$$62.4$$
$$\cdot Y86$$
$$1982$$

Published in 1982 by Praeger Publishers
CBS Educational and Professional Publishing
a Division of CBS Inc.
521 Fifth Avenue, New York, New York 10175 U.S.A.

Printed in the United States of America

ACKNOWLEDGMENTS

I would like to extend my appreciation to Stephen W. Miller and Charles E. Wuller, and particularly to Elwood L. Miller for continuing cheerful help and advice during the writing of the book. Thanks also are due to Richard Hattwick, Director of the Center for Business and Economic Research of Western Illinois University, for generous support of the survey. Finally, a special thanks to my husband, Professor James A. Yunker, for providing secretarial services and unfailing moral support throughout this extended project.

CONTENTS

LIST OF TABLES AND FIGURE

1

INTRODUCTION

A. General Overview and Outline

One of the many problems considered in the literature on accounting aspects of multinational enterprises has been the potential conflict between corporate policies regarding transfer pricing and those regarding performance evaluation of subsidiary managers. It is well-known that several opportunities exist in multinational operation for the enhancement of overall corporate profitability through manipulation of the transfer prices established on transfers of services and goods among the subsidiary companies. However, transfer prices imposed by the parent company that affect the measured profitability of the various subsidiaries complicate performance evaluations of the subsidiary managers. For example, high profitability in a particular subsidiary may partially be the result of transfer-pricing policies and practices that artificially allocate a greater proportion of total subsidiary profit to that particular subsidiary in order to gain tax advantages because the subsidiary is operating in a low-tax country. It is widely agreed in the prescriptive literature that profitability measures used in performance evaluations should be interpreted in the light of transfer-pricing policies and practices, in order to neutralize this potential artificial variation in measured profitability among the subsidiaries.

Until now there have been no systematic empirical investigations of actual practices in multinational corporations regarding transfer-pricing in relation to performance-evaluation policies. But the success of some recent surveys of transfer-pricing policies and objectives in multinational corporations has indicated that many of these companies are willing to respond to fairly detailed inquiries

1

about this aspect of their operations. A questionnaire was written for this study that included inquiries concerning, among other things, performance-evaluation policies in addition to transfer-pricing policies. The survey was carried out in the winter of 1980-81. The survey population consisted of 358 multinational Fortune 500 corporations with headquarters in the United States. Fifty-two usable responses were returned for a 14.5 percent usable-response rate.

Statistical analysis of the responses uncovered many statistically significant interrelationships among the various policy dimensions. However, the single policy interrelationship of greatest immediate interest was between performance-evaluation policy and transfer-pricing policy: clear evidence was found that those firms that tend to use transfer pricing as an instrument for the enhancement of overall corporate profitability more than other corporations place somewhat less emphasis on profit-oriented measures of performance evaluation in their performance evaluations of subsidiary managers. This study has, therefore, produced some evidence that, in this case, actual practices follow the prescriptions of the theoretical literature in the accounting and management journals.

On the other hand, the adjustment made is numerically quite small, even though it is statistically significant. This suggests that while there is a general tendency for companies that make greater use of artificial transfer-pricing methods to place less reliance on profit-oriented performance-evaluation measures, many companies are nevertheless to be found that place heavy reliance on profit-oriented performance evaluation, even though they frequently employ artificial transfer pricing.

While the original impetus for the study was the specific desire to ascertain empirical relationships between transfer-pricing and performance-evaluation policies in multinational corporations, as the study developed its scope was somewhat expanded. This expansion involved two aspects. First, a third area of corporate policy was identified and studied: that of subsidiary autonomy or independence. Contemporary thinking and writing on performance evaluation particularly stresses the close interrelationship between these two areas of policy. In particular, the greater the subsidiary autonomy, the tighter performance evaluation must be in order to maintain the necessary level of control. Interrelationships were thus ascertained among three dimensions of corporate policy rather than just two.

Second, an effort was made to ascertain potential causative factors in the determination of corporate policy in the three areas of interest: subsidiary autonomy, performance evaluation, and transfer pricing. A set of corporate characteristics that might have an effect on the various policy areas were identified. These included the company's size in terms of world sales, the number of subsidiaries in the company, and the short-run profit orientation of the company. These characteristics were systematically related to the various dimensions of policy. As numerous statistically significant results were obtained from this effort, it was sometimes possible to ascertain the roots, in terms of fundamental causation, of various interrelationships among the different policy dimensions.

A succinct outline of the organization of this study is as follows:

I.   Chapter 1—Introduction

    A.   General Overview and Outline

    B.   The Conceptual Framework

        This section introduces the theory of the multinational corporation that guided the construction and analysis of the survey questionnaire. According to this theory, all of the various policy dimensions are causally determined by certain characteristics of the firm that are fixed in the short term, as well as by the firm's external environment. After the general theory is developed, it is applied to the specific problem of accommodating performance-evaluation policy and transfer-pricing practices.

    C.   Nature of the Study

        This section outlines in general terms the methodology by which the survey study illuminates empirically the theoretical view of the multinational corporation set forth in section B above. The items queried in the questionnaire are related to the theoretical categories.

II. Chapter 2—Survey of the Literature

    A.   Decentralization and Performance Evaluation.

        The closely intertwined literatures on decentralization and performance evaluation are surveyed in order to clarify some of the issues and problems upon which the present survey casts empirical light.

    B.   Transfer Pricing

        The same general objective stated immediately above is served by reviewing the literature on transfer pricing. This section also briefly describes the several recent survey studies that have focused on transfer pricing in multinational enterprises.

III. Chapter 3—The Survey Design

    A. Survey Procedure

This section describes the conduct of the survey and argues that the response rate was adequate, given the comprehensiveness of the questionnaire form. Facsimiles of the questionnaire mailings are included.

    B. Statistical Approaches and Tools

This section explains the statistical methodology adopted to analyze the questionnaire responses. The topics covered include the following:

    1. Numerical coding of the responses and the use of mean response and standard deviation of response as descriptive statistics on each subjective judgment item
    2. Use of simple correlation to measure associations between different corporate policy variables
    3. Use of partial correlation to assess causative relationships between corporate policy variables and their determinants in the form of exogenous variables
    4. Construction of a set of summary policy variables
    5. Selection of a set of seven key exogenous variables

Construction of a set of summary policy variables and selection of a set of seven key exogenous variables were necessitated by the large number of different items queried on the questionnaire that could be regarded either as policy variables or exogenous factors. If each of these were treated as separate variables, literally thousands of correlation coefficients could have been obtained. Interpreting such a mass of numbers would have been difficult if not impossible.

    C. Sample Characteristics

This section presents frequency distributions and other numerical information on the firms in the sample in order to indicate as fully as possible the nature of the data base from which the results reported in Chapter 4 are obtained.

IV. Chapter 4—Analysis of Survey Results

    A. Findings on Autonomy

This section reports and comments on

    1. Frequency distributions and descriptive statistics on responses in the area of subsidiary autonomy

2. Partial correlations between the set of summary policy variables in autonomy and the set of seven key exogenous variables

3. Simple correlations within the set of summary policy variables in autonomy

B. Findings on Performance Evaluation

This section reports and comments on

1. Frequency distributions and descriptive statistics on responses in the area of performance evaluation

2. Partial correlations between the set of summary policy variables in performance evaluation and the set of seven key exogenous variables

3. Simple correlations within the set of summary policy variables in performance evaluation

C. Findings on Transfer Pricing

This section reports and comments on

1. Frequency distributions and descriptive statistics on responses in the area of transfer pricing

2. Partial correlations between the set of summary policy variables in transfer pricing and the set of seven key exogenous variables

3. Simple correlations within the set of summary policy variables in transfer pricing

D. Relationships between Autonomy and Performance Evaluation

This section reports and comments on simple correlation coefficients among summary policy variables in the area of autonomy and in the area of performance evaluation.

E. Relationships between Autonomy and Transfer Pricing

This section reports and comments on simple correlation coefficients among summary policy variables in the area of autonomy and in the area of transfer pricing.

F. Relationships between Transfer Pricing and Performance Evaluation

This section reports and comments on simple correlation coefficients among summary policy variables in the area of transfer pricing and in the area of performance evaluation. As the initial purpose of the study was principally to examine this particular area of corporate policy accommodation in multinational enterprise, the analysis and

commentary contained in this section is more extensive
than in the other sections of Chapter 4. Also, additional
statistical results are presented showing some of the statistically significant specific simple correlations among
the disaggregated policy variables that have produced statistically significant correlations among the summary policy variables.

V. Chapter 5—Summary and Conclusions

This chapter reviews the logic and conduct of the survey study,
presents a concise summary of the principal conclusions from
the correlation analysis, and concludes with some customary
caveats concerning statistical inference.

B. The Conceptual Framework

The purpose of this study is to ascertain empirical relationships within and among three particular aspects of corporate policy
in the context of multinational operation. The three policy dimensions of interest are (1) subsidiary autonomy, (2) transfer pricing,
and (3) performance evaluation. The first two of these may be
categorized as specific aspects of a more general area of policy,
namely that of corporate control. The empirical relationships are
assessed by means of data from a survey of multinational corporations with headquarters in the United States. This section develops
the conceptual basis for the survey and its analysis.

The unit of study is the headquarters sector of the multinational corporation. The headquarters (parent) unit faces the problem of specifiying policy in the area of performance evaluation of
subsidiary managers and in the area of corporate control, including
under this general area the two subareas of transfer pricing and
policy regarding the level of autonomy or independence granted to
the managers of the subsidiaries. It is envisioned that the solution
to this problem depends in a systematic way upon the nature of the
environment in which the firm operates and on the given characteristics of the firm. The "given characteristics" of the firm are
those attributes of the firm that cannot be altered in the short run,
including primarily the size and structure of the firm. These characteristics must be regarded by management as more or less in-
variable over a short-run planning period. In the long run, of
course, these characteristics of the firm, no less than its policy,
are determined by the firm's environment.

It is well-known that large multinational corporations are
highly decentralized. However, the freedom of action of the sub-

sidiary managers is not complete. Subsidiary managers must typically make periodic reports on their activities to the parent company. The level of detail in these reports, the extent to which the
actions and decisions of the subsidiary manager must be defended
and justified, and the frequency with which orders are given that
override some aspect or another of established subsidiary behavior
or policy are matters of corporate policy. Among those activities
more likely to be strictly controlled by the parent company are
those directly affecting the operations of other subsidiaries. This
includes physical quantities transferred between subsidiaries and
the pricing of these quantities (transfer pricing).[1]

In addition to control policy, the parent company must establish policies concerning performance evaluation of subsidiary units
and managers.[2] The rewards and punishments meted out to the
subsidiary managers must be tied to some more-or-less objective
and observable set of success criteria such as sales, profits, cost
reductions, innovations, market-share growth, and so on.

Successful policy determination at the headquarters level must
be based on clear recognition of the fact that the corporation is
basically a structured collection of self-interested human individuals.
Successful organizations are those that achieve the best compro-
mise between individual and corporate objectives and that best
harness the individual's self-interested behavior in the interest of
the corporation.[3]

The elements of the corporate policy-determination problem
may be specified as follows: There are two decision-making levels
in the corporation: the parent company and the subsidiary companies. The parent company sets overall performance-evaluation
policy and corporate-control policy (including autonomy policy and
transfer-pricing policy). The subsidiary company sets the levels
of the instrument variables of business enterprise, that is, the dis-
cretionary control variables such as physical outputs, prices, and
so on.

The subsidiary managers who control the instrument variables
desire to maximize their benefits. Benefits depend on outcomes,
through a relationship determined by corporate performance-
evaluation policy. Outcomes in turn depend on instrument variables, corporate-control policy, and environmental factors. Environmental factors include such things as market conditions, competitive pressures, foreign exchange fluctuations, political transi-
tions affecting taxation and the regulatory environment, and so on.
These uncontrollable factors may be termed exogenous or predetermined. Some or all of them are not perfectly predictable, so
that they may also be termed stochastic or uncertain. Thus, the
subsidiary manager must commit to certain instrument-variable

values before the values of the environmental variables that affect outcomes become known. This means that the subsidiary manager confronts a problem in decision making under uncertainty.

The parent company's welfare depends on the outcomes achieved by the subsidiaries. The objective of the parent is to maximize corporate welfare. Its control variables to this end are not normally the basic instrument variables of the subsidiaries, because this would require excessive centralization of decision-making power and make the corporation unworkable and unviable.[4] Instead, the parent's control variables are principally in corporate-control policy and in performance-evaluation policy. Since the outcomes of the subsidiary operations are uncertain (as they depend upon the uncertain environmental factors), the value of corporate welfare is also uncertain. Thus, the parent company also faces a problem in decision making under uncertainty.

This theory of decision making within the corporation implies that all the control variables (instruments such as quantities produced for the subsidiaries and policies in performance evaluation for the parent) are simultaneously causally determined by the given predetermined characteristics of the corporation (its size and structure) and the statistical properties (mean, variance, and so forth) of the uncertain environmental factors (like tax rates, exchange rates, and competition). In a strictly logical sense, therefore, it is not appropriate to speak of causal relationships between the various instrument variables and corporate policies. For example, transfer-pricing policy and performance-evaluation policy are both causally determined by the external factors and the given characteristics of the corporation. Any observed correspondences between them are purely associational and not causative. From the point of view of the individuals involved, however, they will often appear to be causal (for example, "We have such and such a policy on performance evaluation, therefore we must have such and such a policy on transfer pricing").

The objective of this study will be to explore both the causative and the associative relationships pertaining to corporate policy in multinational companies with respect to subsidiary autonomy, performance evaluation, and transfer pricing. Thus, the exogenous factors will be related to various quantitative indicators of policy, and these quantitative indicators of policy will be related to each other. As a result of this effort, empirical information will be obtained on a wide range of problems, issues, and areas of interest in corporate policy.

To illustrate the relevance of the theory of corporate policy making previously sketched, it will now be applied to a well-known, specific problem in corporate administration and policy: the accommodation of transfer pricing and performance evaluation policies.

Profit is normally an important goal for the parent company, and hence subsidiary profitability is normally a principal criterion of performance evaluation of the subsidiary manager. Businesses typically develop plans in which profit goals are a major component. Consider a situation in which the profitability of a particular subsidiary is below goal or expectation. There are three reasons why this may have happened. A critical problem in corporate administration is to disentangle the factors and assess the relative importance of each of the three reasons.

The first possibility is that of manager inefficiency owing either to low effort, low skills, or both. The poor performance of the manager results in the selection of bad values for the instrument variables and, hence, bad values occur for the outcome variables. In this case, the fault lies with the manager, and his suitability for the position is questionable.[5]

The second possibility is an unpredictable and adverse development in some of the environmental variables. The instrument variables may have been set at the appropriate levels, given what was known of the environment, and it was simply bad luck that the environmental variables were perverse. In this case, the fault cannot be attributed to anyone within the corporation, no remedy exists, and the corporation must simply hope for better luck in the future.

These first two possibilities relate to the distinction between performance evaluation of the manager and performance evaluation of the subsidiary. In manager evaluation, the objective is to eliminate (hold constant) the environmental factors so that the specific effects of the instrument variables for which the manager is responsible may be ascertained. In subsidiary evaluation, the objective is to eliminate (hold constant) the instrument variables for which the manager is responsible so that the specific effects of the environmental factors on subsidiary outcomes may be ascertained.[6] Given poor performance by a subsidiary, if the manager evaluation produces a low score and the subsidiary evaluation a high score, the subsidiary is retained and the manager is fired.[7] On the other hand, if the manager evaluation produces a high score and the subsidiary evaluation a low score, then the subsidiary is sold or closed down and the manager moved on to another position within the corporation (assuming that no reason is perceived for the environment to improve and make the subsidiary's operations more successful in the future).[8]

The third possible reason for poor profit performance may lie in corporate policy: performance-evaluation policy may stress other factors to a greater extent than profit or some aspects of control policy may constrain profits. For example, there may be excessive interference with subsidiary decision making by the parent

company, which saps the initiative and self-respect of subsidiary managers, or there may be a transfer-pricing policy that reduces the potential profits of some of the subsidiaries.[9] In this case, the fault lies with the parent company. A change in policy may be contemplated, or, alternatively, the existing policy may be retained as optimal in an overall long-run sense, and the occasional disadvantages it creates may be deemed necessary evils.

The administrative problem of the corporation is in the correct application of existing corporate policies. In the case just cited of subgoal profit performance, the problem for the parent company is to determine the role of each of the three cited possibilities in causing the observed outcome. Only if it appears that the first factor (manager inefficiency) is the primary source of the problem should some sort of action be taken against the manager. The policy problem of the corporation is to determine corporate policies that best enhance the goals of the corporation. In this determination, the ease of administration of the policy is of course an important consideration, but it is by no means the only consideration.

A major concern of this research is with the interaction of performance-evaluation policy with one aspect of corporate-control policy, namely, transfer-pricing policy, within the context of multinational operation. The essence of this interaction will now be addressed as it is seen by business policy analysts.

The considerable stress laid on profit in nearly all business firms should not obscure the fact that corporations typically operate with a multiplicity of goals. Profit is definitely not the only outcome of interest. The relative importance of goals is normally an important political issue within the corporation. Ordinarily there is one school of thought that places a great deal of emphasis on the realization of profit in the short term. This school is customarily opposed by another school less concerned with short-term profit and more concerned with laying a secure foundation for future operations by the corporation.[10] This school is more likely to be concerned with sales growth, innovations, and other manifestations of long-term viability.

Transfer pricing is often viewed as a device for distributing profit among the subsidiaries. It is quite true that in the aggregate, intracompany transfers and subsidiary profits are eliminated when preparing the consolidated financial statements. Some authors have suggested that since the time and effort spent on determining appropriate transfer prices probably has little effect on consolidated income, subsidiaries should be fully autonomous, allowed to trade freely with one another in the marketplace, and free to spend management time better on other problems of the enterprise.[11] Most authors, however, do not regard transfer pricing so lightly. A

given transfer-pricing policy, for example, can materially affect decisions by subsidiaries on buying internally or from an outside vendor and, hence, average unit costs and profits of the subsidiaries and the overall corporation. Transfer prices also affect income tax liabilities, duties, and other amounts levied on subsidiaries operating abroad. These charges can significantly affect the consolidated income of the corporation when the corporation uses the same transfer prices for both tax and accounting purposes.[12]

The selling subsidiary or simply seller is defined as "the subsidiary that produces some physical output or service good and supplies or provides it to another subsidiary in the same company." The buying subsidiary or simply buyer is the subsidiary that accepts, receives, takes, or buys the output in question. Call the selling subsidiary A and the buying subsidiary B.

A high transfer price benefits A by giving it a larger share of profit. By the same token, a high transfer price puts B at a disadvantage. A low transfer price benefits B by giving it a larger share of corporate profit. In so doing, a low transfer price operates to the disadvantage of A. Since the managers of the subsidiaries A and B are judged partially or even mainly on the basis of profits produced by their companies, seller A will want a high price and buyer B will want a low price. In the case of a subsidiary that both buys from and sells to other subsidiaries, the direction of its preference in terms of corporate policy, as opposed to individual transfer prices, will be determined by the relative size of its intracompany sales to its intracompany purchases. If it has a high ratio of sales to purchases, it will tend more to be a type A, or selling subsidiary, and it will tend to favor the policy that leads to high transfer prices.

An issue in semantics should be briefly addressed. The parent company will often try to establish an "equitable" transfer-price policy in order to distribute profits "naturally" among the subsidiaries. A "natural" distribution of profit among the subsidiaries is usually understood to mean the distribution that would occur among them if they were independent and fully autonomous companies. The parent will therefore not think of those prices as being either high or low, but as perhaps medium. But A will tend to regard medium prices as low while B will tend to regard them as high.[13]

The widespread incentive to develop a transfer-pricing policy that results in a natural distribution of profit can be justified not only in terms of equity but also in terms of efficiency. In particular, a natural transfer pricing method that does not arbitrarily redistribute profit facilitates the performance evaluation of managers and subsidiaries. Variations in profit among subsidiaries cannot be attributed to corporate transfer-pricing policy and, hence, are either the result of environmental factors or of managerial performance. This simplification reduces the complexity of the administrative problem of determining the sources of variation in the profitabilities of the various subsidiaries.

The natural division concept (the hypothetical distribution of profit that would occur if all the subsidiaries were operating as independent companies) is an important factor in the adoption of the following important transfer-pricing methods:

Market price
Adjusted market price
Negotiated price
Actual unit full cost plus fixed markup
Standard unit full cost plus fixed markup

To the extent that the parent company for one reason or another desires to achieve an "artificial" division of profit between its subsidiaries, it will tend to use methods that reduce the price as opposed to the above methods, which attempt to duplicate or at least to imitate ordinary market relationships among subsidiaries. These alternative methods include

Actual unit variable cost plus fixed markup
Standard unit variable cost plus fixed markup
Actual unit full cost
Standard unit full cost
Actual unit variable cost
Standard unit variable cost
Marginal cost
Free transfers

The first two of the above do not include fixed cost; the next two do not include the standard markup; the next two do not include fixed cost and the standard markup. Marginal cost at a minimum ignores fixed-cost elements and will be lower than unit variable cost if unit variable cost is declining with output. As a whole, these methods may be categorized as low-price methods, in contrast with the normal-price methods listed previously.

It has already been pointed out that corporate transfer-pricing policy that directly affects the distribution of profit among the subsidiaries complicates performance evaluation, because the profit performance of different subsidiaries becomes less comparable. Those subsidiaries that sell a large amount of output to other subsidiaries (relative to in-kind purchases) will be put at a profit disadvantage through corporate use of any or all of the low-price methods as opposed to the normal-price methods. This will be seen as a matter of inequity to the managers of type A selling subsidiaries. They will tend to protest being judged on the basis of their profits when corporate transfer-pricing policy operates as a profit constraint.

The corporation must therefore have some overriding purpose for concentrating profits in some subsidiaries while depriving other subsidiaries. Some possible purposes apply both to domestic and international operations, while others are peculiar to international operations.

In both domestic and international operations there may be an incentive to concentrate resources in high-potential subsidiaries. The Boston Consulting Group matrix is one well-known categorization of subsidiary companies in terms of their potential.[14] A particular company is classified as high or low in terms of current profit performance and in terms of potential profit growth performance. The idea is that resources should be transferred from the so-called cash cow subsidiaries in the high-current-performance/low-potential-performance category to the so-called rising star subsidiaries in the low-current-performance/high-potential-performance category. One way to accomplish this resource transfer is for the rising star to pay a low transfer price on products transferred from the cash cow and for the cash cow to pay a high transfer price on products transferred from the rising star.

Production considerations, more specifically the existence of economies of scale, may indicate the sensibility of a seemingly artificial transfer price policy. If the selling company A has strong economies of scale in the production of its commodity and it is desired that it produce a large quantity, the transfer price might be held low to encourage other subsidiaries to buy from it. The low price may keep profits in the selling division low, but its large output at a low price may enhance the profits of the other subsidiaries.

The possibilities for utilizing transfer pricing as an active tool for enhancing corporate welfare that exist in domestic operations also exist in international operations, but so also do several additional possibilities.

Nearly all nations tax profits of subsidiary companies, but they do so at different rates. A corporation may use transfer-pricing policy as a means of concentrating profits in subsidiaries operating in low-tax areas. A subsidiary operating in a low-tax country will have its profits enhanced by charging a high price on transfers to subsidiaries in other countries and/or by paying a low price on transfers from other subsidiaries.[15]

Some countries possess currencies the values of which are on a long-run rising trend relative to other currencies, such as the U.S. dollar. A fixed profit in terms of the currency unit of such a country would represent a rising profit in terms of U.S. dollars. At any given time, some countries appear to be more politically stable and hospitable toward foreign investment than other countries. Future operations in such countries are less likely to be heavily taxed, closely regulated, nationalized, or otherwise reduced in value by governmental intervention. An additional incentive for adjusting the transfer price may be to reduce the impact of certain customs duties and tariffs that are assessed on the basis of value rather than physical units.[16]

As a result of the factors enumerated above, it may enhance overall corporate performance to depart from the standard transfer pricing methods that either attempt to duplicate market dealings among independent firms (as in the case of market pricing or negotiated pricing) or to simulate them (as in the case, for example, of full cost plus markup). However, there is a cost involved in such departures in the form of greater complication injected into the determination and administration of performance-evaluation policy. The corporation must weigh this cost along with the benefits in setting its policy.

This specific issue is one of several on which empirical information will be extracted from the survey. Certain key relationships between performance evaluation and transfer-pricing policy will be determined statistically. Particular interest lies in learning whether those corporations that tend to depart from standard market-imitative transfer pricing tend also to adjust downward their emphasis upon profit as a success criterion for subsidiary managers. Such an adjustment would seem likely on theoretical grounds, but this study is the first to offer empirical evidence on the matter.

C. Nature of the Study

While the previous section has developed a conceptual framework for this project, it must be recognized that basically this is an empirical exercise. The conceptual framework is an extremely general theory from which testable hypotheses may be derived only in the broadest and most generalized sense. The theory as explicated in the previous section does not yield any explicit predictions concerning the direction and force of the effects of specific characteristics and environmental factors on specific policy dimensions. Similarly it indicates that relationships should exist among different dimensions of policy, but not how strong such relationships should be or in what direction they should proceed.

On the other hand, the following chapter will present a concise review of the literature regarding the policy dimensions of interest here. Many ideas are circulating in the literature that may be regarded as testable hypotheses. But clearly most of these ideas represent only a small part of the overall policy formulation problem of the multinational corporation. The conceptual framework delineated in the previous section may be conceived as the broad outline of a large jigsaw puzzle, into which various pieces will be fitted that have been suggested by contributions in the literature on decentralization, performance evaluation, and transfer pricing. The idea is to develop a bank of statistical information, guided roughly by the conceptual framework, from which specific results may be drawn out pertaining to notions that have been developed in the literature.

The questionnaire form that comprises the heart of this effort was developed on the bases of the conceptual framework set out in the previous section and the study of the literature on corporate policy in the areas of subsidiary autonomy, performance evaluation, and transfer pricing. There are two principal considerations in designing a questionnaire form. Unfortunately, the considerations work at cross-purposes. In the first place, the questionnaire form should elicit a great deal of valuable information. Second, a questionnaire form should be one to which subjects will respond. The first consideration tends to make questionnaire forms long, elaborate, and complicated. The second tends to make them brief and simple. Deciding upon a happy medium requires delicate judgment. As the questionnaire form used in this study is shown in section III.A., description of it here will be concise and mainly concerned with commenting on certain key issues and problems in the form's construction.

The survey form was entitled "Questionnaire on Transfer Pricing and Performance Evaluation in Multinational Corporations." Although there are three general areas of corporate policy of interest in this study (transfer pricing, performance evaluation, and subsidiary autonomy) the connection between the latter two in ordinary conceptualization of corporate policy making is so close that it was felt that separating them might be confusing to the respondents. Thus, the queries on subsidiary autonomy were included in the section of the questionnaire pertaining to performance evaluation.

Another departure from pure logic, for the purpose of designing a form in which the system would be more readily apparent to the respondents, was the placement of some items pertaining to the external environment of the corporation. These items are in the section on performance evaluation also, because of the obvious bearing of the external environment on performance evaluation of subsidiary managers. In terms of the system developed by the conceptual framework, the external-environment factors are similar in nature to the characteristics of the corporation queried on the first page of the questionnaire form. That is, both corporate characteristics and external environment are factors over which the corporation has no control in the short run but that affect its policy formulation. Of course, in the long run, corporate characteristics may be regarded as under the control of the corporation just as much as are the various dimensions of corporate policy.

It was mentioned above, in the conceptual framework section, that while the actual values of the environmental factors affect the actual outcomes of corporate operations, from the point of view of policy formulation, it is the statistical properties of the random variable environmental factors that are relevant. There is a distinction between formulating policy and living with or carrying out policy, or the actual results that flow from having a certain policy. In the former case, that of policy formulation, the corporation does not know exactly what values the environmental variables are going to take on during the period in which the policy will be in effect. But in order to make a decision on policy, it has to have some idea about the likelihood of certain values for these environmental variables; in other words, it has to have some idea about the statistical properties of the random environmental factors. The two best-known statistical properties are the mean, or basic measure of central tendency, and the variance, or basic measure of dispersion. The mean is the average or most likely value that the variable will take on. The variance is a measure of how much spread there is in the distribution of the variable, that is, how uncertain or unpredictable it is. A high variance indicates that the actual value of the variable is likely to fall further away from the mean value than would be the case if the variance were smaller.

The phraseology settled upon for queries about environmental factors ("How significant are unforeseen changes in this factor in their impact upon subsidiary operations?") was an effort to get at two things at once: importance (mean) and unpredictability (variance). A given factor might be fairly predictable, but it might at the same time be very significant to operations, so that even a very small variation from the expected level could have a strong impact upon operations. Another factor might be inherently less important, yet have a very high level of unpredictability, and so also be considered equivalent to the first factor in its potential impact. In sum, it can be said that the phrasing of the question is an effort to determine whether either or both the mean and the variance of a particular environmental factor has a strong impact on subsidiary outcomes, and hence a strong impact on corporate policy formulation.

Except for a few numerical characteristics at the beginning of the questionnaire form, all items require a multiple choice judgment on the relative importance of a given item in company operations or policy. This approach was dictated by the complexity of large multinational corporations. A given multinational might have 25 or 30 subsidiary companies in its ranks. Obviously, it is not going to evaluate the management of each and every subsidiary in exactly the same manner. Therefore, for example, it would be impossible to answer a question that read, "What is your policy on performance evaluation?" It would also be fairly uninformative to answer a multiple choice question in the form "Do you use such and such a performance-evaluation policy X? Yes—No." The policy X might be used for only two subsidiaries out of a total of 25 or 30. The questionnaire used in this research gives between three and five relative importance evaluations for each item. A company that used a certain performance-evaluation criterion for only two firms out of 25 or 30 subsidiaries would respond that the criterion was "of minor importance" or at most "of some importance." On two general categories of items, the phrasing was varied somewhat from the rule of relative importance or relative significance. Transfer-pricing methods were evaluated in terms of relative usage, and subsidiary autonomy in terms of relative independence of the subsidiary with respect to each of series of business-policy instruments.

Table I.C.1 shows all the items queried by the questionnaire, along with the mnemonics attached to each for purposes of computer analysis of the responses. The table is set up in a format that parallels that of the questionnaire form.

Each item category was prefaced with a question indicating that the interest was in the international aspect of the company's operations rather than in domestic operations. For example, the question heading the part of the questionnaire pertaining to transfer-pricing methods reads "From the point of view of the overall corporation, relatively how often are the following specific transfer-pricing methods utilized for <u>international</u> transfers?"

The phrase "From the point of view of the overall corporation" was reiterated in every question in order to stress that the judgment being requested pertained to tendencies in corporate policy as a whole, rather than to specific policies or procedures precisely applicable to some subgroup of the company's subsidiaries. This, of course, places a considerable strain on the judgmental capacities of the person filling out the form. But there was no other alternative, in that attempting to get at detailed policies pertaining to each of the numerous subsidiaries of the large multinational firms in the

TABLE I.C.1

Items Queried on Survey Questionnaire by Acronym Key

Page 1: Company characteristics

WEMP	Number of employees worldwide (world employees)
FEMP	Number of employees outside U.S. (foreign employees)
WSAL	Sales worldwide, U.S. dollars (world sales)
FSAL	Sales outside U.S., U.S. dollars (foreign sales)
EPO	Value of exports from U.S. subsidiaries to foreign subsidiaries, U.S. dollars (exports)
IMP	Value of imports from foreign subsidiaries to U.S. subsidiaries, U.S. dollars (imports)
MANSD	Number of chiefly manufacturing subsidiaries, domestic
MANSF	Number of chiefly manufacturing subsidiaries, foreign
MARSD	Number of chiefly marketing subsidiaries, domestic
MARSF	Number of chiefly marketing subsidiaries, foreign
DOMSUB	Number of domestic subsidiaries
FORSUB	Number of foreign subsidiaries
NCOUN	Number of countries in which subsidiaries are located
INCD	Number of investment-center subsidiaries, domestic
INCF	Number of investment-center subsidiaries, foreign
PRCD	Number of profit-center subsidiaries, domestic
PRCF	Number of profit-center subsidiaries, foreign
COCD	Number of cost-center subsidiaries, domestic
COCF	Number of cost-center subsidiaries, foreign
CBO	Current business orientation (degree of importance: very high [3], high [2], low [1], very low [0])
CBO1	Short-run profit
CBO2	Long-run profit
CBO3	Growth in sales
CBO4	Increase in market share
CBO5	Employment stability
CBO6	Employee welfare
CBO7	New product development
CBO8	Technological modernization
CBO9	Enhanced social responsibility
CBO10	Other (please specify)

Page 2: Transfer pricing for international transactions

TPGO	Transfer pricing general objectives (dominant objective [3], very important objective [2], somewhat important objective [1], not important [0])
TPGO1	Simplicity and ease of application
TPGO2	Facilitate performance evaluation of managers
TPGO3	Increase overall corporate profit
TPGO4	Increase overall corporate sales
TPGO5	Other (please specify)

18

TPM	Transfer-pricing method (always used [4], often used [3], sometimes used [2], rarely used [1], never used [0])
TPM1	Actual unit variable cost
TPM2	Actual unit full cost
TPM3	Standard unit variable cost
TPM4	Standard unit full cost
TPM5	Actual unit variable cost plus fixed markup
TPM6	Actual unit full cost plus fixed markup
TPM7	Standard unit variable cost plus fixed markup
TPM8	Standard unit full cost plus fixed markup
TPM9	Marginal cost
TPM10	Opportunity cost
TPM11	Dual pricing
TPM12	Mathematical programming optimal price
TPM13	Market price
TPM14	Adjusted market price (market price less selling costs)
TPM15	Negotiated price (unit cost plus negotiated markup)
TPM16	Contribution margin
TPM17	Instrumental price (price set by parent company on a case-by-case basis to benefit the overall corporation)
TPM18	No transfer price (free transfers)
TPM19	Ad hoc transfer price (not based on general policy)
TPM20	Other (please specify)
ITPO	Instrumental transfer pricing objective (degree of importance: high [3], medium [2], low [1], none [0])
ITPO1	Take advantage of economies of scale in production
ITPO2	Provide inexpensive materials for importing subsidiaries
ITPO3	Stabilize the competitive position of a subsidiary
ITPO4	Maintain good relations with host countries
ITPO5	Reduce currency fluctuation losses
ITPO6	Reduce customs duty payments
ITPO7	Reduce sales tax payments
ITPO8	Reduce corporate profits or income taxes
ITPO9	Avoid restrictions on earnings repatriation
ITPO10	Other (please specify)

Page 3: Performance evaluation

PEGP	Performance-evaluation general principles (very important [3], of some importance [2], of minor importance [1], of no importance [0])
PEGP1	Financial measures expressed in U.S. dollars
PEGP2	Financial measures expressed in local currency
PEGP3	Standards set by company-wide performance
PEGP4	Standards set by industry-wide performance
PEGP5	Standards set by economy-wide performance
PEGP6	Standards tailored to specific circumstances

(continued)

Table I.C.1, continued

PESM	Performance Evaluation Specific Measures
PESM1	Ratio of profits to equity
PESM2	Ratio of profits to total assets
PESM3	Ratio of profits to sales
PESM4	Remittances to parent company
PESM5	Net income (profits)
PESM6	Residual income (profits after capital charge)
PESM7	Sales growth
PESM8	Market share
PESM9	Cost reduction
PESM10	Adherence to budgets
PESM11	Meeting plan goals
PESM12	Production technological innovation
PESM13	New product innovation
PESM14	Other (please specify)
INST	Instruments—policy variables of subsidiary managers (degree of subsidiary autonomy: subsidiary determines entirely [4], subsidiary determines mostly [3], parent determines mostly [2], parent determines entirely [1])
INST1	Physical quantities produced
INST2	Price on sales to subsidiaries in same country
INST3	Price on sales to subsidiaries in other countries
INST4	Price on sales outside company
INST5	Quantity of items sold to other subsidiaries
INST6	Quantity of items purchased from other subsidiaries
INST7	Materials and labor purchased in open market
INST8	Major capital investments
INST9	Dividends remitted to parent company
INST10	Major borrowings
INST11	Marketing expenditures
INST12	Research and development expenditures
INST13	Other (please specify)
ENV	Environmental factors—effect of unforeseen changes in (highly significant [3], intermediately significant [2], of little significance [1])
ENV1	Government regulations
ENV2	Raw material and labor costs
ENV3	Overall demand for commodities produced
ENV4	Level of competition
ENV5	Technological conditions
ENV6	Cost of capital (long-term loans)
ENV7	Cost of working capital (short-term loans)
ENV8	Rates of inflation
ENV9	Tax rates
ENV10	Exchange rates
ENV11	Tariffs, customs duties, import quotas
ENV12	Other (please specify)

subject population would have necessitated an impossibly bulky questionnaire form.

The output to be expected from the survey falls into three general categories.

1. Descriptive statistics and frequency distributions on corporate characteristics, environment, and policies;
2. Relationships that may be interpreted as causal among corporate characteristics, environment, and policies;
3. Interrelationships that may be interpreted as associative among corporate policies.

Figure I.C.1 is an attempt to illustrate the theory advanced by the conceptual framework elaborated in the previous section, as applied to the items in the questionnaire form. The number of variables indicated do not include the "other" category listed on the questionnaire form for every subset of variables. It is apparent from inspection of this figure that to present every possible relationship that could be generated by the data would overwhelm the absorptive capacities of any reader of the study. There are 63 specific variables in the policy-dimension category. The different interrelationships on a one-by-one basis thus number 1952 (from the formula for the number of combinations of 63 items taken 2 at a time: [63 x 62] divided by 2). There are 39 variables in the exogenous factor category. If the effect of each and every exogenous factor on each and every policy variable were examined, there would be 2457 (63 x 39) such relationships.

Obviously, in the interest of manageability, some limits had to be placed on the output of the study. It is not so much a matter of computational cost, since a computer was used to generate the results, but of the absorptive capacity of those who might wish to read the study.

There are several ways in which the output may be cut down to size, all of which have been used at some point or another in this study. First, summary variables may be constructed from subsets of similar variables. For example, a variable named TPMMO, indicating "market-oriented transfer-pricing methods," was devised based on TPM6 ("actual full cost plus fixed markup"), TPM8 ("standard full cost plus fixed markup"), TPM13 ("market price"), TPM14 ("adjusted market price"), and TPM15 ("negotiated price"). A smaller number of relationships among the summary variables was then examined. Second, lists were compiled of those statistical relationships that were statistically significant at some level of confidence. Third, some relationships were selected because they have been mentioned in the literature. Finally, the theoretical

FIGURE I.C.1

Schematic Illustration of the Application of the Conceptual Framework
to the Questionnaire Items Listed in Table I.C.1

EXOGENOUS FACTORS

Company Characteristics (28 variables)

Scale and Structure of Operations
WEMP to COCF (19 variables)
Current Business Orientation
CBO1 to CBO9 (9 variables)

Environmental Factors (11 variables)

ENV1 to ENV11 (11 variables)

TOTAL: 39 variables

causative
relationships

ENDOGENOUS POLICY DIMENSIONS

Subsidiary Autonomy Policy (12 variables)

INST1 to INST12 (12 variables)

Transfer-Pricing Policy (32 variables)

Transfer-Pricing General Objectives
TPGO1 to TPGO4 (4 variables)
Transfer-Pricing Methods
TPM1 to TPM19 (19 variables)
Instrumental Transfer-Pricing Objectives
ITPO1 to ITPO9 (9 variables)

Performance-Evaluation Policy (19 variables)

Performance-Evaluation General Principles
PEGP1 to PEGP6 (6 variables)
Performance-Evaluation Specific Measures
PESM1 to PESM13 (13 variables)

TOTAL: 63 variables

associative
interrelationships

22

2

SURVEY
OF THE
LITERATURE

A. Decentralization and Performance Evaluation

Human organizations, from the family through the multinational corporation, attempt to organize the activity of individual human beings toward the achievement of some group objective. The very phrasing that the activity of the individuals has to be "organized" betrays the fact that there is not a perfect consistency between the goals of the individual and the goals of the group. Were there such a symbiosis between individual and group goals, there would be no need of organization, rather, group goals would automatically be achieved as a by-product of each individual's pursuit of his or her own self-interest.

In actual fact, however, there is naturally some opposition of interest between the individual component and the group. In very basic terms, the individual tends to want to put a small amount of effort into achievement of the group's objective and at the same time tends to want to receive a large share of the benefits of the group's activities. To combat this natural tendency toward laziness, selfishness, and so forth, the group must impose some sort of performance evaluation on the individual. The share of the individual in group-achieved benefits is made to depend upon the individual's observable contributions to group objectives. The problem for the group is to decide upon what aspects of group operation are to be left to the individual's determination (the degree of individual autonomy) and what success criteria are to be employed in the evaluation of the individual's contribution to the group (methods of performance evaluation).

model used as a basis for the study provided a general guide to those relationships that were likely to be interesting.

Table I.C.2 provides an overview of some of the output obtained by the study and the location of relevant tables in this study. This is not an exhaustive list of the results presented in the study, but it covers a substantial portion of them.

TABLE I.C.2

Location of Major Output from the Study

Type of Output	Specific Issues	Section	Table
Description of:	Company characteristics		
	Scale and structure	III.C.	1,2,3,4
	Current business orientation	III.C.	5,6
	Environmental factors	III.C.	7,8
	Subsidiary autonomy policy	IV.A.	1
	Performance-evaluation policy	IV.B.	1
	Transfer-pricing policy	IV.C.	1,2,3
Determinants of:	Subsidiary autonomy policy	IV.A.	3
	Performance-evaluation policy	IV.B.	2
	Transfer-pricing policy	IV.C.	4
Interrelationships among:	Autonomy—autonomy	IV.A.	2
	Performance evaluation—performance evaluation	IV.B.	3
	Transfer pricing—transfer pricing	IV.C.	5
	Autonomy—performance evaluation	IV.D.	1
	Autonomy—transfer pricing	IV.E.	1,2
	Performance evaluation—transfer pricing	IV.F.	1,2,3,4

NOTES

1. John M. Stopford and Louis T. Wells, Jr., Managing the Multinational Enterprise: Organization of the Firm and Ownership of the Subsidiaries (New York: Basic Books, 1972), pp. 85-95.

2. The concern in this study will be with performance evaluation of subsidiary managers rather than with performance evaluation of subsidiary units. The distinction between the two is briefly described in page 9 of Section I.B. For an expanded treatment of the two types of evaluation, see David Solomons, Divisional Performance: Measurement and Control (Homewood, Ill.: John D. Irwin, 1965), chap. 3.

3. Cyril Tomkins, Financial Planning in Divisionalized Companies (London: Haymarket, 1973), pp. 6-7.

4. In a few highly integrated and centralized corporations, direct parent control of subsidiary business-policy variables may be the rule rather than the exception. And even in normally decentralized companies, circumstances may occasionally compel temporary parent control of some of these variables.

5. Richard F. Vancil, in his article "What Kind of Management Control Do You Need?" Harvard Business Review 51 (March–April 1973):75-86, draws a distinction between efficiency and effectiveness as follows (p. 82): "One way of contrasting effectiveness and efficiency is to say that efficiency means doing something right and effectiveness means doing the right something." This study addresses only the question of manager efficiency. To determine whether or not a given subsidiary manager is effective, the parent company must rely on a variety of objective and subjective evaluation criteria. To determine these criteria would require indepth interviews with top management. This is an area of potential investigation beyond the scope of this study.

6. James A. Reece and William R. Cool, "Measuring Investment-Center Performance," Harvard Business Review 56 (May-June 1978):36.

7. Solomons, Divisional Performance, p. 59.

8. Ibid., p. 53.

9. Ibid., p. 166.

10. Richard F. Vancil, quoted in John Dearden, "The Case of the Disputing Division," Harvard Business Review 42 (May-June 1964):177.

11. M. C. Wells, "Profit Centers, Transfer Prices, and Mysticism," Abacus 4 (December 1968):174.

12. J. Alex Milburn, "International Transfer Transactions: What Price?" CA Magazine 109 (December 1976):25.

13. Elwood L. Miller, Accounting Problems of Multinational Enterprises (Lexington, Mass.: Heath, 1979), p. 178. Miller emphasizes that while equity is always a consideration in corporate management, this consideration is more important in domestic operations than in international operations. Within the context of international operations, the overall corporate interest is more likely to override considerations of subunit equity. This is owing to the greater abundance of opportunities for profit-enhancing coordination of the subsidiaries' activities in international business.

14. Richard E. Hattwick, The Economic Implications of Corporate Strategic Planning, Western Illinois University, Center for Business and Economic Research Occasional Paper 1980-3 (Macomb: CBER, 1980), pp. 7-11.

15. Ralph L. Benke and James D. Edwards, Transfer Pricing: Techniques and Uses (New York: National Association of Accountants, 1980), p. 121.

16. An important reference for all aspects of transfer-pricing policy in multinational corporations, from considerations of efficiency to legal considerations, is H. C. Verlage, Transfer Pricing for Multinational Enterprises: Some Remarks on Its Economic, Fiscal, and Organizational Aspects (Rotterdam, Netherlands: Rotterdam University Press, 1975).

This general framework has already been applied to the issue of performance evaluation of a subsidiary company in a multinational corporation in Section I.A. The set of observable success criteria includes such things as absolute profit levels, profit rates, cost levels, revenues, market share, innovations, and so on. The set of manager instrument variables includes such things as quantities of materials and labor purchased, prices and quantities produced of output goods, marketing expenditures, research and development expenditures, and so on. The outcomes depend on the values selected by the manager for the control or instrument variables just enumerated, but they depend in addition on two other factors. The first factor encompasses the environmental variables, some of which at least will be uncertain (that is, their values will not become known for sure until after the values of certain key control variables have already been set). The second factor is corporate policy. The problem for the corporation is to develop corporate policy so that overall corporate welfare is maximized subject to the constraint that the subsidiary managers will be maximizing their own welfare subject to the set of constraints relevant to them in the form of existing corporate policy and environmental conditions.

There are several basic issues that emerge from this concept of the corporate policy problem with respect to performance evaluation. First, the corporation must decide upon the level of autonomy to be extended to the subsidiary managers. Second, it must determine those outcomes that will be relevant to performance evaluation and how they will be weighted relative to one another. Third, the corporation must decide upon other policies that affect variables concerned with performance evaluation. Finally, the corporation must attempt to achieve a clear understanding of how environmental variables affect the performance measures of the subsidiary company, and also how its own corporate policy affects these measures.

Table II.A.1 is a tabular representation of the overall performance-evaluation concept applied to various types of subsidiaries. Each type of subsidiary has a certain specified area of freedom (set of control variables), has other variables that are specified by the parent company (variables predetermined by the parent company), and finally is evaluated according to some specific objective. It has to be recognized that this is a schematic portrayal. No particular subsidiary is likely to be considered completely a cost center or completely a profit center. In addition, there is always some degree of parent intervention with the control variables. For example, even an investment center is likely to have to justify a proposed investment, at least very broadly, before it may be undertaken.

TABLE II.A.1

Schematic Description of Various Center Concepts

Type of Center	Subsidiary Control Variables	Variables Predetermined by Parent Company	Objective
Cost center	Prices and quantities of inputs	Prices and quantities of outputs	Minimize cost
Expense center (for example, service department)	Prices and quantities of inputs	Budget	Maximize services to corporation
Revenue center (for example, sales department)	Prices and quantities of inputs	Quantities to be sold Budget	Maximize sales revenue
Profit center	Prices and quantities of inputs and outputs	Investment	Maximize profit
Investment center	Prices and quantities of inputs and outputs and investment	None	Maximize return on investment

A great deal of performance-evaluation literature is concerned primarily with issues of administration. The broad recommendations of this literature are straightforward enough. The following are thoroughly agreed-upon principles for developing and administering a performance-evaluation system:

1. The criteria and procedures of performance evaluation ought to be developed in as explicit and as detailed a manner as is feasibly possible, given the complexity of the problem and the variety of circumstances that may arise. Both the superior and the subordinate should have as clear an idea of what is involved in performance evaluation as is possible—before the evaluation period gets under way.

2. The criteria of performance evaluation should be as sophisticated and as accurate as possible. The standards should be relevant and the measurement should be precise.

3. It is best to use several criteria of performance rather than just one. This is because of the risk of a bad decision based on a single criterion. There is a fairly good chance that at any one point in time some particular criterion will indicate inferior performance, while others will indicate acceptable performance. Only if a large number of criteria simultaneously indicate poor performance is the performance likely to be, in fact, poor.

One of the strongest recommendations to be found in the literature is this last injunction, to avoid single measures of performance in favor of multiple criteria. The disadvantages of application of a single standard are in actual fact simply the problems of performance evaluation in general. But it is perceived that these problems are less likely to apply to a whole range of criteria than to a single one. The problems include the following:

1. Bad short-term performance may not indicate bad long-term performance. In fact, under some circumstances, poor short-term performance may be a means of accumulating resources toward good long-term performance.

2. Bad performance may be owing to environmental variability or corporate policy over which the subsidiary manager has no control. In the case of environment, the problem may be temporary or it may be permanent. In the latter case, the subsidiary would be evaluated poorly and perhaps sold or shut down, but this would not (or should not) be regarded as a stain on the reputation of the manager.

3. Bad performance may be the result of errors in the application of the criterion. The wrong variables may be measured, or the right variables may be inaccurately measured.

A good example of the literature on performance evaluation is the controversy that surrounds the use of return on investment (ROI) as a criterion of performance. One author, John Dearden, has practically made a career out of published assaults on the ROI criterion.[1] Robbins and Stobaugh, Mauriel and Anthony, and Solomons have endorsed the Dearden objections.[2] These authors' objections to ROI are a catalogue, broken down and finely subdivided, of the objections to single-criterion performance evaluation enumerated above.

According to these authors, owing to past performance, different subsidiaries are likely to have different ROI goals. Thus, a subsidiary with a 25 percent goal might reject a project with a 20 percent rate of return while another subsidiary with a 15 percent goal undertakes it. But assuming the cost of investment resources to both subsidiaries is less than the expected return, both projects ought to be undertaken. This situation would be a manifestation of error in the application of the criterion. Residual income (profits after capital expense) is the appropriate objective. It should be recalled, however, that if the capital invested and the interest rate paid for investment capital are the same for both subsidiaries, then a ranking of both subsidiaries' list of projects by ROI will match the ranking by residual income. It is also an error to rate a project in relation to return received on prior projects. Project returns should be related only to their present costs: in other words, projects should be evaluated on a marginal basis rather than an average basis.

Further, ROI evaluation reduces consideration of what is often a highly complex situation to a single, unrealistically simple criterion. This is an expression of the nearly universal condemnation of single-criterion rating systems. It is based, as we have mentioned, on the fallibility of any single measure and the idea of "risk spreading" through consideration of multiple criteria.

ROI evaluation can lead to manipulation of fixed-asset purchases in order to reduce the denominator and, thus, increase the ROI ratio. This is an inversion of the point made above concerning the possibility that bad short-term performance may not imply bad long-term performance. Presumably the artificial curtailment of the subsidiary's capital investment will have an adverse effect in the long run.

It is further argued that the computation of the investment base varies widely from one company to another, complicating the comparison of ROI figures from different subsidiaries. This is a problem of measurement. Presumably all subsidiaries in a single corporation should be using similar methods of computing the capital investment base. If they are not, and yet are compared on the basis of ROI, this would constitute an error in the application of a criterion.

Also, no single ROI standard can be applied to subsidiaries with different potentials. This is another reference to the fact that the primary interest of the corporation is in residual income from subsidiaries, not in the rate of return. This is a slight reworking of the first objection above. It is also a reference to the environmental factors that differ from one subsidiary to the next and that must be taken into account before performance of subsidiary managers can be compared.

When a subsidiary has high ROI on its previously undertaken projects, it may be reluctant to undertake new projects with lower ROI that will bring down the average ROI on all projects. This is another reference to the error of making average rather than marginal evaluations of projects.

Finally, short-run increases in ROI can adversely affect the long-run profit potential of the subsidiary. This is closely allied to artificial curtailment of subsidiary investment.

The use of ROI as a basic measure of performance is not without its defenders, in spite of the several vigorous assaults that have been made upon it. Reece and Cool, in their 1978 study, take the view that the criticisms of ROI are mostly hypothetical in nature and/or highly exaggerated as to their impact, so that under most circumstances, a sophisticated application of ROI analysis will still yield a large amount of fairly valuable and comparable information concerning the operations of a set of subsidiary companies.[3]

However, the desirability of using multiple performance-evaluation criteria has been argued by a great many authors in addition to Dearden. For example, Wilkinson in 1975, Parker in 1979, Tse in 1979, and Miller in 1979.[4] The idea of multiple goals is of course not new. In fact, some early authors expressed concern over the possible problems inherent in extremely complex and multifaceted performance-evaluation systems. Dean, in a 1957 study, was concerned that the evaluation system not be too complex in order to facilitate efficient administration. He felt that profit should be the predominant criterion and the other criteria should be regarded as ancillary factors, regarded mainly for the purpose of casting light on the expected future or long-term profitability of the subsidiary.[5] Ridgway was concerned that multiple goals can cause the manager to become uncertain about relative importance of goals.[6] There can be a very adverse effect on the morale and performance of a manager if his own perception of relative importance of goals happens to differ from the perception in the corporate headquarters. In this context, some authors, Wilkinson and Ferrara, for example, have been particularly concerned with consistency in criteria.[7] They are concerned that criteria not be changed in the middle of an evaluation period, because of the adverse effect on managerial morale. Wilkinson also stresses the desirability of attainable goals. Excessive and unrealistic goals may actually put too much pressure on the manager so that he becomes anxious, frustrated, and ineffective.

The problem of consistency in goals is directly related to the problem of the length of the evaluation period. Some authors, like Dearden, say that the usual one-year period is too short, particularly with respect to large investment projects.[8] As time passes and the condition of the corporation itself changes, the overall goals are likely to change, and as a consequence, the parent company will want to alter the evaluation system applied to the subsidiary managers. But, if the evaluation period is very lengthy, there is not much flexibility in this respect.

The current tendency in the prescriptive literature on performance evaluation is to recommend a comprehensive system of budgets and goals tailored to the specific environmental circumstances of each subsidiary.[9] Some authors have particularly stressed the effect of environmental factors on subsidiary outcomes and have urged that these factors be duly assessed before setting performance goals for the various subsidiaries.[10] One environmental factor that has recently received a great deal of attention has been exchange-rate fluctuations. The recent amplification of variability in exchange rates has created the problem of whether and how to edit out the effects of such fluctuations prior to performance evaluation.[11] Some authors argue that qualitative environmental factors that cannot be numerically measured (for example, the political stability of a host country) should be taken into account along with the quantitative factors, such as ROI, in assessing performance.[12] Other authors have pointed out that the accounting measures prepared for outside users of financial reports are often not very appropriate for performance evaluation.[13]

Not every contribution has been prescriptive of the goals-and-budgets approach, even though it is predominant. As mentioned above, some authors have expressed qualms about overcomplexity of the evaluation system, which may divert attention from maximum performance with respect to the really important bottom-line measures of performance. In a technical contribution, Itami has demonstrated a possible problem with the goals and budgets evaluation system; namely, if penalties are applied for departures from these goals, the manager may avoid actions that would probably increase bottom-line measures, because there is some risk that they would cause subgoal performance in some less-important measures. Itami is only making a point in a technical way that is already fairly obvious from intuition: that goals and budgets do have the disadvantage of reducing the manager's flexibility, which may lead to the loss of some opportunities that otherwise would have been realized.[14]

Most of the literature has been concerned with specific issues in the determination and administration of corporate policy on performance evaluation. Not that many authors have gone deeply into the basic problem itself of a divergence in interest between the corporation as a whole and the individual subsidiary manager. For the most part, there are the usual vague pronouncements about "goal congruence," which is the term commonly used to suggest a desirable solution to the conflict of interest problem. The corporation is supposed to set its policy so that self-seeking behavior on the part of the subsidiary manager will lead to outcomes favorable to the corporation. For example, if a corporation wants to receive profits, the material rewards bestowed upon the subsidiary managers should be at least to some extent dependent upon the profits earned by their subsidiary companies. The real problem lies in how much performance evaluation should depend on profit relative to other criteria. For example, doing research and development now will reduce current profit, but it may lead to product or production technology innovations that will increase future profits. Obviously, the subsidiary manager should be rewarded both for current profits and for activity that increases the likelihood of future profits. But exactly how much of the current reward should be allocated on the basis of current profit and how much on the basis of research and development effort? The nontechnical literature is, perhaps necessarily, somewhat vague about the answers to questions like this. Some authors have made explorations along technical lines that may prove fruitful at some future point. The recent article by Demski and Feltham in the <u>Accounting Review</u> is an example of this work. [15]

It was indicated above that one of the questions in performance-evaluation policy concerns the relationship of this policy area to other corporate policy areas. The two other corporate policy areas of interest in this study are subsidiary autonomy and transfer pricing. With respect to autonomy (decentralization), the prescription is that subsidiary managers should only be held accountable for that over which they have control. [16] That is, not only should environmental factors be accounted for before the performance evaluation is completed, but also the effect of other corporate policies which constrain the flexibility of the subsidiary manager. For example, if a new product innovation is unsuccessful in the market, the subsidiary manager is perhaps not to blame if corporate policy prevented him from undertaking anything more than a vestigial advertising campaign. The general message is that it is only fair to be very stringent with respect to performance evaluation if the corporation at the same time allows the subsidiary managers a great deal of flexibility in discharging their responsibilities. Not everyone,

however, is insistent upon the virtues of decentralization and dele-
gation of authority. Larsen, for example, maintains that the usual
effect of decentralization is to foster excessive individualism among
the subsidiary managers, and this individualism operates as a se-
vere constraint on what can be accomplished through coordination
of the activities of the subsidiaries.[17] This is just one more reference to the ancient and not totally solvable problem of goal congruence, which has been treated herein as a problem in compromis-
ing individual with group interests and objectives.

There has also been a certain amount of literature that has
specifically addressed problems of coordination between performance-
evaluation policy and transfer-pricing policy. One important rule is
that if a subsidiary is to be treated as a profit center and evaluated
principally, if not totally, on the basis of its profit, the transfer
price it charges to other subsidiaries ought to make some allowance
for the profit it would presumably make were it selling outside the
company. On the other hand, if a subsidiary is in fact a natural cost
center, a cost-based transfer price may be used—if the subsidiary
is then evaluated as a cost center.[18] These issues will be developed
further in the following section on transfer pricing.

B. Transfer Pricing

In a totally centralized organization such as a single factory or
a single household, physical transfers of goods and services are
mostly free. Modern large corporations, whether they operate only
domestically or also internationally, are of course far from being
as centralized as a factory or household. Total centralization of
decision-making power in a complex and diverse human organization
would result in a virtual paralysis that would soon eliminate the
organization from the scene. "Most large corporations are the result of past mergers between various companies that were at one
time wholly independent." From the social point of view, there has
been a centralization of authority. But from the point of view of the
parent firm, the progression has been from more centralization in
the days when operations were less complex and diverse to less
centralization in the present day.

The previously independent companies are now treated as distinct subsidiaries whose performance is, at least to some degree,
independently evaluated. Transfer pricing refers to the pricing of
flows of physical goods and services among subsidiaries of the same
overall corporation. As the pricing of these flows is likely to have
some bearing on the criteria used in performance evaluation, it is
obvious that there are political ramifications in the setting of

transfer-pricing policy within the corporation. Any given policy will favor some subsidiaries and disfavor others.

In very rough terms, transfer-pricing methods may be divided into two general categories: those methods that attempt to duplicate or imitate the ordinary market relationships that existed between the subsidiary companies before they became merged together in the corporation, and those methods that are aimed at a substantial modification of the physical and financial flows that would be taking place if the subsidiaries were not merged together. The former transfer-pricing methods will be referred to as market-oriented. The latter may be variously referred to as low transfer-pricing methods, ad hoc methods, or instrumental methods, to use the term coined in the first chapter. The basic idea behind the latter methods is to take advantage of the fact that the subsidiaries are centrally controlled. Those who oppose these methods are likely to complain that they represent overcentralization of authority within the corporation, that their advantages are overestimated, and that their costs are underestimated.

Market-based transfer-pricing methods are probably more extensively applied than instrumental methods. They have several important advantages.

They are simple and easy to understand.
They keep the complications involved in performance evaluation to a minimum.
They tend to keep conflict between the various subsidiaries to a minimum.
They are basically consistent with the usual taxation and regulatory environments in the United States and abroad.
Under some circumstances, they have theoretical efficiency properties.

Departures from market-based transfer pricing may be justified on a number of grounds.

There is no alternative, since no outside market exists for the product.
It is necessary to take advantage of economies of scale in the production of certain goods and services.
It is necessary to shift resources from low-potential to high-potential subsidiaries.
It is necessary to shift profits from high-tax areas to low-tax areas.
It is necessary to reduce transfer taxes.

The last three of these are particularly applicable to multi-national operation. In the context of domestic operation, high-potential and low-potential subsidiaries are usually distinguished on the basis of the likely growth of the market for their products. This factor is often relevant in the international sphere as well, but so also are some additional important factors. The various nations in which a given multinational corporation operates are likely to have very different prospects in terms of future trends in exchange-rate values, inflation, and political stability. A parent company may wish to concentrate resources in those subsidiaries located in countries that are expected to be politically stable, experience low rates of inflation, and have appreciating exchange rates relative to other currencies. Tax rates are also likely to vary substantially among different countries, so that an appreciable reduction in the overall tax burden on the corporation may be achieved by establish-ing transfer prices that concentrate profits in lower-tax countries. Finally, flows of resources among countries are likely to involve a tax cost in terms of customs duty payments. Judicious selection of transfer prices may be able to reduce these obligations as well.

The transfer-pricing policy of the corporation impinges on the outcomes of the subsidiary companies in the same way as an exoge-nously determined environmental factor. Therefore, the transfer-pricing policy of the corporation has to be taken into account just as much as more obvious factors such as changes in prices, tax rates, and so on in the performance evaluation of subsidiaries and sub-sidiary managers. This additional complication injected into per-formance evaluation is a powerful disincentive to the use of transfer pricing as a positive policy tool for instrumental purposes.

A great deal of literature on transfer pricing falls into the general category of prescription; that is, it recommends and defends a particular method in preference to alternatives. Within the gen-eral category of prescriptive literature, one may distinguish the technical literature from the nontechnical. The technical literature relies on more-or-less sophisticated economic, graphic, and mathematical tools, while the nontechnical literature leans more on intuition, verbal argumentation, and numerical examples.

A considerable amount of technical literature has been con-tributed by economists. The contributions of Hirschleifer are es-sentially an effort to apply the economic efficiency principles per-taining to operation of the economy as a whole to the decentralized corporation.[19] Hirschleifer views the decentralized corporation as a small economy of interacting firms. Just as marginal cost pricing is efficient in a social sense, so also will it achieve the maximum efficiency within the corporation. There has been a stream of literature since Hirschleifer that has developed this basic idea in terms of successively more complicated models of the corporation. Dean, Ronen, and McKinney have all covered the case of decreasing cost subsidiaries; Horst and Bond have investigated cases of differential tax rates and tariffs in multinational operation; and Gould has examined the marketing costs of using an outside market.[20]

Another branch of the technical literature has been contributed mainly by mathematically oriented operations analysts and management scientists. The distinction between this literature and the economics-based literature is that the former makes heavy use of mathematical programming as a means of solving the problem rather than representing the solution in calculus or graphic terms, as is the case in the economic literature on transfer pricing. Some of the many contributors to the programming literature on transfer pricing include Samuels, Rutenberg, and Kanodia;[21] Bailey and Boe have produced a recent survey of the programming-based literature.[22]

There is not as yet in the business real world much usage (at least conscious usage) of transfer-pricing formulas devised by economists and mathematical programmers. The mathematical complexity of these recommended methods serves as an effective deterrent to their comprehension and application. This is not to say that the methods in extensive use in the real world are necessarily more effective than would be the application of the theoretical methods; there is the possibility that real-world methods in actual fact approximate closely (through a kind of trial-and-error process) the potential results from theoretical methods. Abdel-Khalik and Lusk, in their survey of the analytical approaches, make some interesting observations on the question of the relationship between the theoretical methods and the actual methods reported to be commonly used by real-world companies.[23]

Turning to the non-technical prescriptive literature, it may be noted that many of the methods that have been advocated in this literature are in fact popularizations of certain methods that have previously been put forward in the theoretical literature. For example, Onsi, Holstrum, and Sauls recommend opportunity cost, and Goetz recommends incremental cost (marginal cost).[24]

Some authors, in a quandary as to the advantages and disadvantages of the various methods, attempt to realize the best of both worlds by use of dual pricing. One set of prices would guide the internal allocation while another would be used for performance evaluation.[25]

Benke and Edwards have made a major recent effort to draw together many strands of the prior literature into a practical prescription.[26] This National Association of Accountants-sponsored study develops a menu of several basic methods for utilization under different circumstances. All the methods can be viewed as adaptations of a single method involving lost contribution margin, which is essentially the opportunity-cost idea.

Many other contributions are concerned generally with matters of prescription but do not become so explicit as to recommend a specific method of transfer pricing. One important category is the behavioral literature on the relationship between transfer-pricing policy and intracorporate conflict. General considerations on the topic are provided by Watson, Baumler, Stanley, and Dascher.[27] An actual example of a case of corporate conflict stemming from transfer-pricing policy has been written up by Dearden.[28] A primary concern of this literature is with the reduction of intracorporate conflict generated by the use of transfer pricing for instrumental purposes.

The relationship between transfer pricing and intracorporate conflict has been a major factor in specific recommendations made by some authors. For example, Menge is very insistent that under no circumstances should a subsidiary be forced to buy inside the corporation.[29] Several authors have proposed negotiated prices as being the most consistent with internal corporate harmony in the absence of outside markets for the product.[30] It is not surprising that Lambert's 1979 survey study indicated that lower corporate conflict was achieved with market-price transfer pricing than with negotiated price.[31]

A number of articles have been concerned with developing a transfer-pricing policy that is consistent with the tax and regulatory environment. For example, Stone, Keegan, and Seghers all consider the restricting influence of Section 482 of the Internal Revenue Service Code.[32] Stone has also considered the relationship between antitrust enforcement and transfer pricing.[33]

Another theme in the applied literature has been the transfer prices that should be charged by a subsidiary that is a natural cost center, either because no outside market exists for the product or because the product is produced under decreasing cost conditions. Generally, the recommendation is that such a subsidiary should not be turned into a "pseudo-profit" center by having it charge full cost plus a markup.[34] Rather, it is more efficient to evaluate it as a cost center, have it charge only cost, and thus reap the benefits that are inherent in the special circumstances. Another frequently reiterated point is that if instrumental purposes are pursued to a significant extent by a corporation through its transfer-pricing practices (such as in the case of obtaining the advantages of natural cost centers just mentioned), there should be a correspondingly reduced emphasis upon profit in performance evaluation.[35]

There are important additional avenues through which corporate goals may be pursued by transfer pricing in the international context relative to the domestic context. General considerations relating to the pros and cons of using transfer pricing for instrumental purposes in multinational corporations have been offered by several authors, including Shulman, Solomons, Milburn, Choudhury, and Madison.[36] Although the costs and problems of using transfer pricing as an active tool in the pursuit of corporate goals are given due consideration, the general tenor of this writing is that there are a lot of unrealized opportunities for profit enhancement out there in the real world, and that multinational corporations should devote greater energy to taking advantage of these opportunities. One does occasionally encounter a protest, however, that in practice the complications and hazards involved in attempting to use instrumental transfer pricing are too great for this tool to be very important.[37]

Many efforts have been made to develop empirical information on transfer-pricing policies and practices in real-world corporations by means of questionnaire and/or interview surveys. A partial list of studies over the last 15 years that are either highly or totally oriented to reporting the results of extensive surveys is as follows: National Industrial Conference Board, Mautz, Piper, Greene and Duerr, Arpan, Business International Corporation, Okpechi, Emmanuel, Milburn, Miller and Kim, and Tang.[38]

These survey studies are very diverse. Mautz considers transfer pricing as a component of an overall financial reporting and control system; Okpechi is concerned with the effect of transfer pricing policies on intracorporate conflict; Tang is concerned with international variations in transfer pricing policy; and Milburn is concerned with the legal and political constraints on use of transfer pricing for instrumental purposes.

At the risk of oversimplification, it may be said that the empirical survey literature suggests the following generalizations regarding real-world transfer-pricing policies:

1. Companies are likely to use a variety of transfer-pricing methods, but the dominant single method remains market price.

2. Companies generally view transfer pricing as more than an accounting formality. They think of policy formulation with respect to transfer pricing as an important component of overall company policy formulation toward the end of realizing corporate objectives.

3. Transfer pricing is an important source of political conflict within the corporation, and even undeviating use of market price for transfers does not entirely eliminate this conflict.

4. Multinational companies are generally conscious of the potential opportunities that exist for enhancement of corporate goals through active manipulation of transfer prices, but they are also strongly cognizant of the obstacles to successful manipulation in the legal and regulatory environment and in the general variability and unpredictability of the business environment.

5. There is certainly some utilization of transfer prices for instrumental purposes in the real world, but the indications are that this is not considered one of the principal instruments of business policy by most corporations.

NOTES

1. John Dearden, "Problems in Decentralized Profit Responsibility," Harvard Business Review 38 (May-June 1960):79-86; idem, "Limits on Decentralized Profit Responsibility," ibid. 40 (July-August 1962):81-89; Bruce D. Henderson and John Dearden, "New System for Divisional Control," ibid. 44 (September-October 1966): 144-60; and John Dearden, "The Case against ROI Control," ibid. 47 (May-June 1969):124-35.

2. Sidney M. Robbins and Robert B. Stobaugh, "The Bent Measuring Stick for Foreign Subsidiaries," Harvard Business Review 51 (September-October 1973):80-88; idem, Money in the Multinational Enterprise: A Study of Financial Policy (New York: Basic, 1973); John J. Mauriel and Robert N. Anthony, "Misevaluation of Investment-Center Performance," Harvard Business Review 44 (March-April 1966):98-105; David Solomons, Divisional Performance: Measurement and Control (Homewood, Ill.: Richard D. Irwin, 1965); and idem, "Intracorporate Conflict in International Business," in Topics in Accounting and Planning, ed. Richard Matterrich (Vancouver, Canada: University of British Columbia, 1972), pp. 1-15.

3. James S. Reece and William R. Cool, "Measuring Investment-Center Performance," Harvard Business Review 56 (May-June 1978):28-30.

4. J. W. Wilkinson, "The Meanings of Measurements," Management Accounting 57 (July 1975):49-52; Lee D. Parker, "Divisional Performance Measurement: Beyond an Exclusive Profit Test," Accounting and Business Research 9 (Autumn 1979):309-19; Paul S. Tse, "Evaluating Performance in Multinationals," Management Accounting 60 (June 1979):21-25; and Elwood L. Miller, Accounting Problems of Multinational Enterprises (Lexington, Mass.: Heath, 1979), pp. 195-96.

5. Joel Dean, "Profit Performance Measurement of Division Managers," The Controller 25 (September 1957):423-24, passim.

6. V. F. Ridgway, "Dysfunctional Consequences of Performance Measurements," Administrative Science Quarterly 1 (September 1956):240-47.

7. Wilkinson, "The Meanings of Measurements"; William L. Ferrara, "Accounting for Performance Evaluation and Decision Making," Management Accounting 58 (December 1976):13-19.

8. John Dearden, "Appraising Profit-Center Managers," Harvard Business Review 46 (May-June 1968):80-87.

9. Henderson and Dearden, "New System"; Robbins and Stobaugh, "Bent Measuring Stick."

10. Tse, "Evaluating Performance."

11. Gerald J. Dietemann, "Evaluating Multinational Performance under FAS No. 8," Management Accounting 61 (May 1980): 49-55; J. A. Garda, "The Measurement of Financial Data in Evaluating Overseas Managerial Efficiency," International Journal of Accounting 12 (Fall 1976):13-17; Rhuwan Bushan, "Effects of Inflation and Currency Fluctuation," Management Accounting 56 (July 1974):17-19; Duane Malmstrom, "Accommodating Exchange-Rate Fluctuations in Intercompany Pricing and Invoicing," ibid. 59 (September 1977):24-28.

12. Parker, "Divisional Performance Measurement."

13. A. G. Hopwood, "An Empirical Study of the Role of Accounting Data in Performance Evaluation," Journal of Accounting Research Supplement, 1972, pp. 156-93; Solomons, Divisional Performance, pp. 114-15.

14. Hiroyuki Itami, "Evaluating Measures and Goal Congruence under Uncertainty," Journal of Accounting Research 13 (Spring 1975):91-120.

15. Joel S. Demski and Gerald A. Feltham, "Economic Incentives in Budgetary Control Systems," Accounting Review 53 (April 1978):336-59.

16. Solomons, Divisional Performance, p. 59; M. C. Wells, "Profit Centers, Transfer Prices, and Mysticism," Abacus 4 (December 1968):174-81.

17. Raymond L. Larson, "Decentralization in Real Life," Management Accounting 55 (March 1974):28-32.

18. Ralph L. Benke and James D. Edwards, Transfer Pricing: Techniques and Uses (New York: National Association of Accountants, 1980).

19. Jack Hirschleifer, "On the Economics of Transfer Pricing," Journal of Business 29 (July 1956):172-84; idem, "The Economics of the Divisionalized Firm," ibid. 30 (April 1957):96-108; and idem, "Internal Pricing and Decentralized Decisions," in Management Controls: New Directions in Basic Research, ed. C. Bonini, R. Jaedicke, and H. Wagner (New York: McGraw-Hill, 1964).

20. Joel Dean, "Decentralization and Intracompany Pricing," Harvard Business Review 33 (July–August 1955):65–74; J. Ronen and G. MacKinney, "Transfer Pricing for Divisional Autonomy," Journal of Accounting Research 8 (Spring 1970):99–112; Thomas Horst, "The Theory of the Multinational Firm: Optimal Behavior under Different Tariff and Tax Rates," Journal of Political Economy 79 (September–October 1971):1059–72; Eric W. Bond, "Optimal Transfer Pricing when Tax Rates Differ," Southern Economic Journal 47 (July 1980):191–200; and John R. Gould, "Internal Pricing in Firms when There Are Costs of Using and Outside Market," Journal of Business 37 (January 1964):61–67.

21. J. M. Samuels, "Opportunity Costing: An Application of Mathematical Programming," Journal of Accounting Research 3 (Autumn 1965):182–91; David P. Rutenberg, "Maneuvering Liquid Assets in a Multinational Company: Formulation and Deterministic Solution Procedures," Management Science 16 (June 1970):B671–83; and Chandra Kanodia, "Risk Sharing and Transfer-Price Systems under Uncertainty," Journal of Accounting Research 17 (Spring 1979): 74–98.

22. Andrew D. Bailey, Jr., and Warren J. Boe, "Goal and Resource Transfers in the Multigoal Organization," Accounting Review 51 (July 1976):559–73.

23. A. Rashad Abdel-Khalik and E. J. Lusk, "Transfer Pricing—A Synthesis," Accounting Review 49 (January 1974):8–23.

24. Mohammed Onsi, "A Transfer-Pricing System based on Opportunity Cost," Accounting Review 45 (July 1970):535–43; Gary L. Holstrum and Eugene H. Sauls, "The Opportunity-Cost Transfer Price," Management Accounting 54 (May 1973):29–33; and Billy E. Goetz, "Transfer Prices: An Exercise in Relevancy and Goal Congruence," Accounting Review 42 (July 1967):435–40.

25. Paul W. Cook, Jr., "New Technique for Intracompany Pricing," Harvard Business Review 4 (July–August 1957):74–81.

26. Benke and Edwards, Transfer Pricing.

27. David J. H. Watson and John V. Baumler, "Transfer Pricing: A Behavioral Context," Accounting Review 50 (July 1975): 466–74; Curtis H. Stanley, "Cost-Basis Valuation in Transactions between Entities," ibid. 39 (July 1964):639–47; Paul E. Dascher, "Transfer Pricing: Some Behavioral Observations," Managerial Planning 21 (November–December 1972):17–21.

28. John Dearden, "The Case of the Disputing Divisions: How Should Decentralized Organizations Handle the Interdivisional Pricing Problem?" Harvard Business Review 42 (May–June 1964): 158–59, passim.

29. John A. Menge, "The Backward Art of Interdivisional Transfer Pricing," Journal of Industrial Economics 9 (July 1961): 215–32.

30. James M. Fremgen, "Transfer Pricing and Management Goals," Management Accounting 52 (December 1970):25-31; James H. Schaub, "Transfer Pricing in a Decentralized Organization," ibid. 59 (April 1978):33-42; and S. P. Dagher, "What's the Price when a Company Buys from Itself?" Administrative Management 37 (May 1977):32-33, passim.

31. David R. Lambert, "Transfer Pricing and Interdivisional Conflict," California Management Review 21 (Summer 1979):70-75.

32. Willard E. Stone, "Tax Considerations in Intracompany Pricing," Accounting Review 35 (January 1960):45-58; Warren J. Keegan, "Multinational Pricing: How Far Is Arm's Length?" Columbia Journal of World Business 4 (May-June 1969):57-66; and Paul D. Seghers, "How to Set and Defend Intercompany Prices under Section 482 Regulations," Taxes 47 (October 1969):606-22.

33. Willard E. Stone, "Legal Implications of Intracompany Pricing," Accounting Review 39 (January 1964):38-42.

34. David A. Dittman, "Transfer Pricing and Decentralization," Management Accounting 54 (November 1972):47-50; Ralph L. Benke and James D. Edwards, "Should You Use Transfer Pricing to Create Pseudo-Profit Centers?" ibid. 62 (February 1981):36-39, 43.

35. Irving L. Fantl, "Transfer Pricing—Tread Carefully," CPA Journal 44 (December 1974):42-46; Wells, "Profit Centers, Transfer Prices, and Mysticism."

36. James S. Shulman, "When the Price Is Wrong—By Design," Columbia Journal of World Business 2 (May-June 1967): 69-76; idem, "Transfer Pricing in the Multinational Firm," European Business (January 1969):46-54; Solomons, "Intracorporate Conflict"; J. Alex Milburn, "International Transfer Transactions: What Price?" CA Magazine 109 (December 1976):22-27; Nandan Choudhury, "Transfer-Pricing Practices: Room for Debate," Accountancy (England) 90 (August 1979):105-6; and Roland Madison, "Responsibility Accounting and Transfer Pricing: Approach with Caution," Management Accounting 60 (January 1979):25-29.

37. Walter Lamp, "The Multinational Whipping Boy," Financial Executive 44 (December 1976):44-46.

38. National Industrial Conference Board, Interdivisional Transfer Pricing (New York: National Industrial Conference Board, 1967); Robert K. Mautz, Financial Reporting by Diversified Companies (New York: Financial Executives Research Council, 1968); A. G. Piper, "Internal Trading," Accountancy (England) 80 (October 1969): 733-36; James Greene and Michael G. Duerr, Intercompany Transactions in the Multinational Firm (New York: Conference Board, 1970); Jeffrey S. Arpan, International Intracorporate Pricing: Non-American Systems and Views (New York: Praeger, 1972);

Business International Corporation, Setting Intracorporate Pricing Policies (New York: Business International Corporation, 1973); Simeon O. Okpechi, "Interdivisional Transfer Pricing: A Conflict Resolution Approach" (Ph. D. diss., Ohio State University, 1976); Clive Emmanuel, "Transfer Pricing: A Diagnosis and Possible Solution to Dysfunctional Decision Making in the Divisionalized Company," Management International Review 17, no. 4 (1977):45-59; J. Alex Milburn, "International Transfer Pricing in a Financial Accounting Context" (Ph.D. diss., University of Illinois, 1977); Seung L. Kim and Stephen W. Miller, "Constituents of the International Transfer-Pricing Decision," Columbia Journal of World Business 14 (Spring 1979):69-77; Roger Y. W. Tang, Transfer-Pricing Practices in the U.S. and Japan (New York: Praeger, 1979); and idem, "Canadian Transfer-Pricing Practices," CA Magazine, 113 (March 1980):32-38.

3

THE
SURVEY
DESIGN

A. Survey Procedure

The population for this research consisted of those 358 corporations on the Fortune 500 list with international operations.
Volume 2 of the American Encyclopedia of International Information: Directory of American Firms Operating in Foreign Countries
was used to determine whether or not a particular corporation on the
Fortune 500 list was engaged in international operations. Dun and
Bradstreet's Million Dollar Directory and Standard and Poor's
Register of Corporations were consulted to determine the names of
the officers of each corporation so that the survey inquiries could
be personally addressed.

If a controller was listed, the survey was sent to that person.
Otherwise it was sent to the financial vice president (sometimes the
two positions are consolidated). In a few cases in which neither the
controller nor the financial vice president was listed by name, the
survey form was sent to the president of the company.

The questionnaire form provided spaces for the name of the
person filling out the form as well as the name and headquarters
address of the company. It was made clear that filling in these spaces
was optional, in case the company wished to participate anonymously.
However, as an incentive for participation, a large box was provided
labeled "Check here if you desire a summary report on this study."
A parenthetical note than pointed out that in order to distribute the
summary report, it would be necessary to know the name and address of the company. The majority (60 percent) of those responding
did indicate a desire to receive the summary report and provided
their own name and their company affiliation.

On November 14, 1980, a trial mailing was sent out to 60 companies. Returns seemed adequate, and so on December 17-18, 1980, the remaining survey forms were sent out. A total of 358 companies were contacted.

The mailing to each company consisted of the following items:

A mechanically typed, personally signed cover letter from the principal investigator
The survey form
A one-page project description
A postpaid return envelope provided by the Center for Business and Economic Research of Western Illinois University
Two brochures issued by the College of Business at Western Illinois University, described as sponsor information

The cover letter, survey form, and project description are reproduced as the Questionnaire Mailing Packet at the end of this chapter. The two brochures included one describing the American Business Hall of Fame, an undertaking of Western Illinois University's College of Business, and another describing the programs conducted by the Executive Development Center of the College of Business. These additional enclosures were intended to demonstrate that the principal investigator on the project was affiliated with a pro-business university, in an effort to reduce the suspicion with which business executives often regard requests for information from academics.

A follow-up mailing to those companies that had not yet responded was sent out on February 5, 1981. This mailing included the following:

A mechanically typed, personally signed cover letter from the principal investigator (shown in the Questionnaire Mailing Packet)
The survey form
A postpaid return envelope provided by the Center for Business and Economic Research of Western Illinois University
Selected information from responses received as of that time

This last enclosure consisted of a copy of the survey questionnaire form with the box for each response to a subjective item filled in with the percentage of companies (of the 33 usable returns as of that date) selecting that response. This information was provided in an effort to make the firms feel some obligation to respond and to emphasize that the information was being requested for statistical purposes and not to obtain details on specific companies.

The cut-off date for incorporating responses into the statistical data base was April 1, 1981. By that date, some 77 responses had been received, of which 52 represented usable responses that were incorporated into the statistical data base.

Several companies (25) responded to the mailing but declined to complete the questionnaire. The reasons given for not doing so included

1. Company policy is to not fill out questionnaires because too many are received (13 companies)
2. Foreign operations are so limited that a response would be of no value to the study (4 companies)
3. They have no international transfers (2 companies)
4. They are not a multinational company (2 companies)
5. Year-end closing precluded participation (1 company)
6. Information requested is confidential (1 company)
7. Information requested is too extensive (1 company)
8. Foreign affiliates are not controlled by the company (1 company)

The 52 usable responses constitute 14.5 percent of the 358 questionnaire forms sent out. While the percentage return is relatively small, it should be recognized that the sample size in absolute numbers is quite substantial. The 52 companies in the sample provided detailed information on their policies in regard to subsidiary autonomy, transfer pricing, and performance evaluation. Considering the amount of detail requested of the firms by the questionnaire form and the fact that the limited resources available for this project did not permit telephone campaigns and personal interview travel, the response rate has to be regarded as satisfactory.

Included in the sample are several giant multinational corporations including

Dow Chemical Company
Monsanto, Incorporated
Dupont Chemical Company
Owens-Corning Fiberglass
  Corporation
Union Oil Company
Standard Oil of Indiana
Xerox Corporation
R. J. Reynolds Industries

Avon Products, Incorporated
General Motors Corporation
American Motors Corporation
Kaiser Aluminum Company
Control Data Corporation
Burroughs Corporation
International Telephone and
  Telegraph

All of the above are multibillion dollar corporations that responded to the survey, identified themselves, and requested a summary report of the study. The companies represent a cross-section from a number of industries. In addition to these giant companies, many smaller and less widely recognized companies also responded, so that the sample covers a range of sizes as well as a range of industries.

Response rates below that achieved in this project are often observed in published research. For example, in 1979 Kim and Miller reported results in the Columbia Journal of World Business based on 30 usable responses to a mailing of 342 questionnaire forms, for a usable response rate of only 8.8 percent.[1] Moreover, the questionnaire utilized in the Kim-Miller study only required responses to nine judgmental items and it contained no objective-information items. In contrast, the present study asked for responses to 83 judgmental items and 19 objective-information items, for a total of 102 items.

When higher response rates are achieved than were obtained in this project, there are often two factors involved. The first is that the questionnaire form is much simpler. For example, Tang's 1979 study received 247 usable responses from a mailing of 669 inquiries, for a usable response rate of 36.9 percent.[2] But Tang's questionnaire only concerned transfer-pricing methods and objectives, whereas the present study queried companies concerning transfer-pricing methods and objectives, subsidiary autonomy policies and performance-evaluation policies. It appears that Tang's questionnaire contained only about 40 items compared with the more than 100 on the questionnaire of this study.

The second factor is that the study may be endorsed and/or sponsored by some quasi official professional association. For example, the Financial Executives Research Council supported a major research effort directed by R. K. Mautz and reported in the thick volume Financial Reporting by Diversified Companies.[3] A sample of 254 companies was selected and subjected to strong pressure to return a questionnaire form, including personal visits from representatives of the project and invitations to special meetings to explain the nature and importance of the survey. This intensive (and expensive) pressure resulted in a total of 86 usable responses from the 254 companies in the sample, for a usable response rate of 33.8 percent. However, the full sample mailing of about 2,700 questionnaire forms brought in a total of 412 usable responses, for a usable return rate of 15.2 percent, which is only slightly better than the 14.5 percent rate achieved in this project. Except for the first 254 companies, the remainder of the sample in the Mautz study did not receive special pressure to fill out the questionnaire form (apart from the usual written appeals and exhortations). While it is significant that a questionnaire form with the backing of the prestigious Financial Executives Research Council only did marginally better with respect to usable return rate than the questionnaire form of this project, it is only fair to point out that the questionnaire form used in the Mautz study was of monumental proportions. It filled 26 closely printed pages, queried literally hundreds of items, and frequently required written statements rather than mere checking of boxes or filling in of numbers in the specified spaces. Mautz and his associates themselves estimated that the time requirement to fill out the form conscientiously was in excess of two full working days. Had such a form not had the backing of some semiofficial agency, the response rate would almost certainly have been negligible.

Some of the empirical investigations on transfer pricing and other dimensions of corporate policy in the published literature seem blissfully unconcerned with the concept of the response rate. For example, Greene and Duerr, in reporting on a study of multinational transfers done for the National Industrial Conference Board, say that 130 executives responded to their inquiry but nowhere indicate how many executives were contacted.[4] Some other well-known studies are apparently content with very small data bases. For example, the recent National Association of Accountants study of transfer pricing by Benke and Edwards relied for empirical input on personal interviews with some 19 corporate controllers.[5] Not only is 19 a fairly small number in absolute terms, but nowhere did Benke and Edwards indicate the basis for their selection. In the absence of information to the contrary, it is imagined that the basis for selection was rather casual.

In the light of these points, it would seem that a sample of 52 corporations, many of them major forces in the corporate world, that represents 14.5 percent of the contacted population constitutes a substantial data base from which results may be drawn with some degree of confidence.

B. Statistical Approaches and Tools

Some 19 items on the first page of the questionnaire form required numerical answers (for example, number of domestic investment-center subsidiaries). It was expected that the person filling out the form might not have ready access to the actual figures for some of the queries. In an effort to mitigate this deterrent to filling out the form, there was a statement on the form itself inviting the respondent to give estimates if some of the actual figures would be difficult to ascertain. Moreover, the cover letter stressed that a partially completed form would be infinitely more valuable to the project than no form at all. This approach deviates from the insistence on complete response to be found in some questionnaire studies.

It undoubtedly improves the response rate, although there is a cost in lost observations on some variables.

The majority of the items on the questionnaire form required multiple choice judgments of relative importance. Not counting the "other" item available for every subset of items, there was a total of 83 subjective-judgment items. Response to these items was very good. In a few rare instances where no judgment of relative importance was made by the respondent, the lowest relative-importance value was scored in order to obtain a complete record for the respondent on the relevant variable.

For the numerical company characteristics, on the other hand, several of the respondents took the cover letter at its word and provided incomplete information. A value of 99 was recorded for missing numerical information, and in statistical operations using a variable for which some observations were recorded as 99, the computer was instructed to select only those cases for which a 99 was not recorded for that variable. The incomplete data on some of the variables do operate as a constraint on what can be obtained from the study, but the larger response rate that was achieved by not insisting on complete response to every item enables greater confidence to be placed in those results that are obtainable.

The responses to the subjective-judgment items were coded as numerical values, the higher number indicating the higher importance (or greater applicability, greater usage, and so on as the case may be). The usual scale was in the nature of 3 for "very important," 2 for "important," 1 for "less important," and 0 for "not important." For one subset of items (transfer-pricing methods), the scale went from 4 down to 0, and for another subset (environmental factors), it went from 3 to 1. The numerical values assigned to each relative-importance judgment are shown in Table I.B.1, and also in those tables that report frequency distributions of responses to particular item subsets.

It could certainly be argued that for some respondents at least, the subjective appreciation of the significance of very important as opposed to simply important is not, for example, 3 as to 2. Be this as it may, the assignment of numerical values to relative-importance judgments is very widespread both in the research literature and in everyday applications.[6] Computer programs for survey analysis, as, for example, in student evaluation of teachers, assume that subjective judgments that are in principle noncomparable among individuals will be represented by numerical values, and the information is recorded as numerical values and processed in a numerical manner.

The motivation for recording judgmental responses in numerical terms is indeed very strong. Translation of these responses into numbers permits the computation of mean response and standard deviation of response, which greatly facilitates comparisons of perceived relative importance or relative usage of different items. It also opens the door to a wide range of statistical analysis techniques that require numerical information, such as correlation and regression, for developing and understanding relationships among different items. To sum up, it would seem that the consensus is that the loss in data accuracy from numerical translation of judgmental variables is far outweighed by the improvement in our ability to analyze the data.

It has already been indicated (see Section I.B. above, particularly Table I.C.2) that the statistical output from this study falls mostly into three general areas: (1) descriptive information; (2) causative relationships between exogenous factors and policies; and (3) associative relationships among corporate policy variables. The statistical methods utilized for each of the three areas will now be briefly discussed.

Descriptive Information

Numerical information concerning scale and structure of operations is presented in Section III.C., "Sample Characteristics." This information is presented exclusively in the form of frequency distributions.

Responses to subjective-judgment items are covered in Sections III.C. (current business orientation and environmental variability), IV.A. (subsidiary autonomy policy), IV.B. (performance-evaluation policy), and IV.C. (transfer-pricing policy). For each item, the frequency distribution of responses is given as well as the mean response and standard deviation of the response. For example, if 10 percent of the sample selected response 3, 60 percent selected response 2, 15 percent selected response 1, and 15 percent selected response 0, the mean response would be 1.65 (=(.1 x 3) + (.6 x 2) + .15 x 1) + (.15 x 0)). The standard deviation is the square root of the sum of squared deviations from the mean. For example, a response of 3 deviates from the mean of 1.65 by 1.35. If these deviations are squared (to eliminate the problem that some deviations are plus and others are minus), multiplied by the proportion with that deviation, and summed, the result is "variance." The standard deviation is the square root of the variance. For example, the variance in the case above is .319125 (= (.1 x 1.35^2) + (.6 x $.35^2$) + (.15 x $-.65^2$) + (.15 x -1.65^2)), and the standard deviation is .564811... (= $\sqrt{.319125}$).

The higher the mean, the greater the relative importance of the item to the respondents in the sample. The higher the standard deviation, the greater the dispersion of judgments concerning relative importance. Since all items in a particular subset have the same relative-importance numerical rating system, the means and standard deviations within these subsets can be compared with one another in order to assess the relative importance and relative dispersion of the different items.

Causative Relationships

Most variables are affected causally not by one variable but by each of a set of variables. A classical statistical problem is that of taking a set of actual data that reflects the causal effects of each of a set of independent variables $(X_1, X_2, \ldots, X_n)$ operating simultaneously on one dependent variable (Y) and assessing the individual causative effect of each independent variable on the dependent variable as if the other variables had not varied and thus confused the actual statistical information.

Two important techniques for tackling this problem are multiple regression analysis and partial correlation analysis. Multiple regression analysis estimates a linear relationship between the dependent variable Y and a set of independent variables. The coefficients of each of the independent variables (called regression coefficients) are computed so as to minimize the sum of squared deviations between the estimated values of the independent variable Y^e from the linear relationship $Y^e = a + b_1 X_1 + b_2 X_2 + \ldots + b_n X_n$, and the actual observed values Y^a. Another way to put it is that the linear relationship produces an estimated value of the dependent variable (Y^e) and the regression technique computes the coefficients of this relationship so as to maximize the simple correlation coefficient between the estimated value and the actual value.

Partial correlation utilizes multiple regression as a stepping-stone. The idea is to determine the effect of X_1 (for example) on Y under circumstances where all the other independent variables $(X_2$ to $X_n)$ are held constant. Y is regressed on X_2 to X_n, and then X_1 is also regressed on X_2 to X_n. The "residuals" (errors, deviations, and so forth) are then computed—the differences between the estimated Y^e and X_1^e from the regressions and respectively the actual observed values Y^a and X_1^a. Then the simple correlation coefficient is taken between these residuals. The residuals represent the variation in Y and X_1 purged, as it were, of the influence of X_2 through X_n. The result of their correlation is thus the same as the hypothetical result of a simple correlation of Y and X_1 values drawn from a sample for which there had been no change in the X_2 through X_n variables (as for example in a controlled laboratory experiment).

Needless to say, these statistical methods are not without serious weaknesses. In order for them to produce a true insight into reality, certain conditions ought to be present in the real world from which the data are drawn. Often these conditions are not actually present or are present only in a very imperfect way. As a result, statistical results must be interpreted with great caution. In general, one does not accept a statistical result as being a true representation of reality unless there are some additional grounds, either in terms of intuitive plausibility or theoretical reasoning, for supposing that the result is valid.

Associative Relationships

In order to assess associative relationships, this study relies mostly upon the simple, or "Pearson product moment," correlation coefficient. Technically, a simple correlation coefficient between a variable Y and another variable X is the covariance of X with Y divided by the product of the standard deviations of X and Y. The covariance of X and Y, in turn, is the sum of the products of all the deviations of Y from its means for each observation times the deviations of X from its mean for the corresponding observation. If Y tends to vary positively (directly) with X (high values of X tend to be associated with high values of Y and low values of X with low values of Y), the covariance will tend to be a high positive number. If Y tends to vary negatively (inversely) with X (high values of X tend to be associated with low values of Y and low values of X with high values of Y), the covariance will tend to be a small negative number (that is, a negative number high in absolute value).

While this study was in its formative stages, a considerable number of regressions were performed. But for reasons to be indicated, not much of this output will be reported here. In general, the results of the partial correlations will be reported rather than the results of the regressions. Simple correlation coefficients and partial correlation coefficients share several properties. In fact, they are basically the same thing. The simple correlation coefficient is a measure of association between two variables Y and X. The partial correlation coefficient is a measure of association between Y and X holding one or more other variables constant.

It is in the nature of a correlation coefficient, whether simple or partial, to vary within the range of –1 to +1. If the coefficient is negative, it indicates an inverse association between X and Y: low values of X mean high values of Y and vice versa. If the coefficient is positive, it indicates a positive association between X and Y: low values of X mean low values of Y, and high values of X mean high values of Y. The square of the correlation coefficient, R^2, represents the proportion of variation in Y that can be explained, in the sense of statistical association, in terms of variation in X. For example, a simple correlation coefficient of .60 has an associated R^2 of .36. That is, 36 percent of the variation in Y can be attributed, in a statistical sense, to variation in X.

With respect to the question of whether an observed correlation represents causation (X actually affects Y) or merely association (X and Y are being simultaneously affected in the same direction or in opposite directions by a third variable Z), it must be said that this is a matter of interpretation as influenced by some kind of theory, whether of a common sense or a sophisticated nature. It must be recognized that a high simple correlation coefficient and a high corresponding R^2 do not necessarily imply causation. By the same token, a low simple correlation coefficient and a low R^2 do not necessarily imply absence of causation. A common situation is that simple correlation will fail to perceive what may be a strong causal relationship between a given variable X_1 and Y because of the confusing effects of other variables $(X_2 \ldots X_n)$ that also affect Y. As indicated above, multiple regression and partial correlation are attempts to penetrate this screen of complex interaction. However, they do not always work. For example, there may be a confusing variable actually present in the data set on which no information has been collected. The resultant inability to hold this variable constant in a statistical sense may abrogate the possibility of perceiving certain causal realities by means of multiple regression or partial correlation that are nonetheless fully valid relationships.

If a correlation coefficient is close to zero, it means that the data indicate little statistical association between X and Y, and that apparently X has little effect on Y (associational or causative). There is the problem of what is meant, in a statistical sense, by the phrase "close to zero." This problem motivates the concept of a test of significance. Although technically what is tested in most statistical tests of significance is the null hypothesis that there is no association between X and Y, the user automatically tends to think of it as testing for the existence of such a relationship. It is purely a matter of semantics. In rejecting the null hypothesis that there is no association, one is thereby accepting the alternative hypothesis that there is an association.

In a test of significance, one is asking the question of whether or not the estimated coefficient (simple correlation coefficient, partial correlation coefficient, regression coefficient, or R^2) is sufficiently far away from zero to justify presumption of a true relationship (either causational or associative in nature). In order to answer such a question, some assumptions about underlying statistical realities must be made. The results of the tests reported here are from the Statistical Package for Social Scientists (SPSS)

program series. They are based on the assumption that the variables
themselves, or the disturbance terms in the case of regression, are
normally distributed. This assumption is by far the most common on
which statistical tests of significance are based. On the basis of this
assumption, an estimate can be developed of the standard deviation
of the estimated coefficient (since it is based on random observations
it is itself random). This estimate of the standard deviation is called
the standard error. A t-statistic can then be computed as the ratio
of the coefficient value to its standard error. The t-statistic enables a test of the null hypothesis that X and Y are not related. If
the null hypothesis is true, then the t-statistic has a certain probability distribution, and the probability of obtaining the observed t-
statistic can be ascertained. If this probability is low, the implication is that the null hypothesis is not in fact true and that indeed a
relationship does exist between X and Y.

The format chosen for presenting the results of this study lists
a computed statistical coefficient with its significance level placed
immediately beneath in parentheses, as, for example,

-.2411

(.082)

Presume this is a simple correlation result. The negative sign on
the correlation coefficient indicates a negative association between
X and Y. The parenthesized number beneath the correlation coefficient is the probability that one would be incorrect if one presumed
that the indicated relationship does actually hold. Technically speaking, this is the probability of Type I statistical error—the error of
incorrectly rejecting a true hypothesis. (The hypothesis referred to
in the technical definition is the null hypothesis that no relationship
exists.) Therefore, in this case, if one presumed that an inverse
association held between X and Y, there would be an 8.2 percent
probability (82 chances out of 1,000) of being mistaken, and in fact
no such relationship exists. Obviously, the lower the number in the
parentheses, the better the odds for presuming that a relationship
exists.

The two benchmark standards for significance in customary
statistical practice are 5 percent (.050) and 1 percent (.010). These
are of course very conservative standards. For purposes of this
study, more generous guidelines for statistical significance are allowed. Most of the variables measured by the questionnaire are
subjective judgments. Even the numerical answers to the first page
items are much more likely to be estimates than checked and verified
figures. As a result, a higher degree of random variation is likely
to be present in the data than in the average statistical project. To
compensate for this, a statistical coefficient will be regarded as significant when its significance level falls to the level of 20 percent or

below (.200 or below). At a 20 percent significance level there is still an 80 percent confidence level. That means that there is an 80 percent chance (4 out of 5) of being right when accepting that a given relationship truly exists.

The customary practice in reporting significance levels in this study will be to designate those significance levels between .200 and .100 with a single asterisk, between .100 and .050 with a double asterisk, and below .050 with a triple asterisk. For example:

.0436	.1210	.2369	.4073
(.387)	(.148)*	(.076)**	(.035)***

This practice will better enable the reader to focus on those statistical relationships out of a set of results.

It was mentioned in section I.B that an overwhelming abundance of potential statistical coefficients may be computed based on the 102 different items queried by the questionnaire. Some means was needed to reduce the number of coefficients to be considered. It is not, to repeat, a matter of computational cost; the modern computer is tireless in churning out thousands upon thousands of results. But there is no way to analyze such a mountain of results in a sensible fashion.

There are certain statistical methods available, principally factor analysis, for allowing a data set to form variable subsets or groups on the basis of sophisticated statistical association criteria. These methods could not be applied to this project, however, because of the small number of observations available.

The problem of small number of observations is compounded by the fact that for some company characteristic variables, an incomplete set of observations was obtained. The need to have a reasonable number of observations means that some of these variables were deleted from the analysis.

A principal means of coping with the indicated problem was to define a much smaller number of summary policy variables, each one based on a subset of similar policy variables, and to specify a limited number of key exogenous variables. Many of the results presented below show relationships among and between components of the set of summary policy variables and the set of key exogenous variables.

Table III.B.1 shows the composition of the summary policy variables. Each summary policy variable is defined as the average of the policy variables listed immediately beneath it. To some extent, this procedure is based on the notion that the component variables are substitutes for one another and to some extent that they are complements. For example, PESMPR (profit-oriented performance-

TABLE III.B.1

Construction of Summary Variables by Acronym Key

Subsidiary Autonomy
   INSTA   All instrument variables
      INST1   Physical quantities produced
      INST2   Price on sales to subsidiaries in same country
      INST3   Price on sales to subsidiaries in other countries
      INST4   Price on sales outside company
      INST5   Quantity of items sold to other subsidiaries
      INST6   Quantity of items purchased from other subsidiaries
      INST7   Materials and labor purchased in the open market
      INST8   Major capital investments
      INST9   Dividends remitted to parent company
      INST10   Major borrowings
      INST11   Marketing expenditures
      INST12   Research and development expenditures
   INSTSR1   Short-run instruments (first measure)
      INST1   Physical quantities produced
      INST4   Price on sales outside company
      INST7   Materials and labor purchased in the open market
   INSTSR2   Short-run instruments (second measure)
      INST1   Physical quantities produced
      INST4   Price on sales outside company
      INST7   Materials and labor purchased in the open market
      INST11   Marketing expenditures
   INSTLR   Long-run instruments
      INST8   Major capital investments
      INST10   Major borrowings
      INST12   Research and development expenditures
   INSTIN   Internal-transaction instruments
      INST2   Price on sales to subsidiaries in same country
      INST3   Price on sales to subsidiaries in other countries
      INST5   Quantity of items sold to other subsidiaries
      INST6   Quantity of items purchased from other subsidiaries
Performance Evaluation
   PEGPD   Dollar-oriented performance evaluation
     PEGP1   Financial measures expressed in U.S. dollars
   PEGPO   Objective performance-evaluation criteria
     PEGP3   Standards set by company-wide performance
     PEGP4   Standards set by industry-wide performance
     PEGP5   Standards set by economy-wide performance
   PEGPS   Subjective performance-evaluation criteria
     PEGP6   Standards tailored to specific circumstances
   PESMPR   Profit-oriented performance-evaluation criteria
     PESM1   Ratio of profits to equity
     PESM2   Ratio of profits to total assets

(continued)

Table III.B.1, continued

PESM3	Ratio of profits to sales
PESM4	Remittances to parent company
PESM5	Net income (profits)
PESM6	Residual income (profits after capital charge)
PESMG	Growth-oriented performance-evaluation criteria
PESM7	Sales growth
PESM8	Market share
PESMC	Cost-reduction performance-evaluation criterion
PESM9	Cost reduction
PESMBG	Budget-goal-oriented performance-evaluation criteria
PESM10	Adherence to budgets
PESM11	Meeting plan goals
PESMI	Innovation-oriented performance-evaluation criteria
PESM12	Production technological innovation
PESM13	New product innovation

Transfer Pricing

TPMMO	Market-oriented transfer-pricing methods
TPM6	Actual unit full cost plus fixed markup
TPM8	Standard unit full cost plus fixed markup
TPM13	Market price
TPM14	Adjusted market price (less selling costs)
TPM15	Negotiated price (unit cost plus negotiated markup)
TPMLO	Low transfer-pricing methods
TPM1	Actual unit variable cost
TPM2	Actual unit full cost
TPM3	Standard unit variable cost
TPM4	Standard unit full cost
TPM5	Actual unit variable cost plus fixed markup
TPM7	Standard unit variable cost plus fixed markup
TPMIN	Instrumental transfer-pricing method
TPM17	Instrumental price (price set on a case-by-case basis to benefit the overall corporation)

Environment

ENVA	Overall environmental variability
ENV1	Government regulations
ENV2	Raw material and labor costs
ENV3	Overall demand for commodities produced
ENV4	Level of competition
ENV5	Technological conditions
ENV6	Cost of capital (long-term loans)
ENV7	Cost of working capital (short-term loans)
ENV8	Rates of inflation
ENV9	Tax rates
ENV10	Exchange rates
ENV11	Tariffs, customs duties, import quotas

evaluation specific measures) is based on PESM1 to PESM6, all of
which are profit-oriented performance-evaluation specific measures.
A firm that places high reliance on profit in the performance evaluation of subsidiary managers should indicate high importance on at
least one of the measures shown in PESM1 to PESM6. Owing to its
particular accounting conventions, it may place a great deal of stress
on ratio of profits to equity and only a little on ratio of profits to
assets. In this sense, the ratio of profits to equity may be thought
of as a substitute for the ratio of profits to assets. But at the same
time, a firm that emphasizes profit may well indicate that both ratios
are important, so that a high ranking of ratio of profits to equity will
tend to be associated with a high ranking of ratio of profits to assets.
In this sense, the alternative ratios may be regarded as complementary to one another. As far as the entire sample is concerned, the
complementary tendency is apparently more important than the sub-
stitutive tendency. This may be ascertained from an inspection of
Table III.B.2, which shows the simple correlation coefficients among
all component variables of PESMPR. There are several positive and
significant correlations. In fact, among the 15 different and nontrivial correlation coefficients (that is, not counting correlations of
PESM1 to PESM6 variables with themselves and not double counting
PESMi by PESMj along with PESMj by PESMi), there are nine correlation coefficients that are significant at the 10 percent significance
level or better. Only two of the correlation coefficients in the set
are negative, and those are statistically insignificant.

The summary policy variables represent dependent variables
in a causative process in which company characteristics and external
environment play the role of exogenous independent variables. The
objective in deciding upon a set of key exogenous factors is to develop
a relatively small and manageable set of variables that will nevertheless fully exploit the data set and represent a fairly comprehensive set of explanatory variables. The following are the variables
that were selected for this purpose:

Acronym	Variable
WSAL	World sales
SUB	Number of subsidiaries
NCOUN	Number of countries in which the company operates
FSUBR	Ratio of foreign subsidiaries to total subsidiaries
FSALR	Ratio of foreign sales to total sales
CBO1	Short-term profit orientation (current business objective 1)
ENVA	Environmental variability

TABLE III.B.2

Simple Correlation Coefficients among Profit-Oriented Performance-Evaluation Specific Measures

	PESM1	PESM2	PESM3	PESM4	PESM5	PESM6
PESM1	1.000					
PESM2	.3542 (.005)***	1.000				
PESM3	.2430 (.041)***	.3126 (.012)***	1.000			
PESM4	.2237 (.055)**	.0392 (.391)	.0534 (.354)	1.000		
PESM5	.2894 (.019)***	.0367 (.398)	.1931 (.085)**	.2196 (.059)**	1.000	
PESM6	.2060 (.071)**	-.0295 (.418)	.0438 (.380)	-.0471 (.370)	.3143 (.012)***	1.000

Code: PESM1 Ratio of profits to equity
PESM2 Ratio of profits to total assets
PESM3 Ratio of profits to sales
PESM4 Remittances to parent company
PESM5 Net income (profits)
PESM6 Residual income (profits after capital charge)

Note: Parentheses indicate significance level. Sample size is 52 corporations.

The rationale for including each one of these variables will now be briefly discussed.

World sales (WSAL) is a basic measure of the scale of the company. It is universally recognized that the physical scale of a company is likely to have some effect on its policy.

Number of subsidiaries (SUB), when controlling for the financial scale of the organization with world sales (WSAL), is a measure of its structural complexity, diversity of product lines and activities, and so on.

Number of countries (NCOUN) reflects the complexity of the company's international commitment, as distinct from the diversity of its business operations, which has already been covered in "number of subsidiaries."

Ratio of foreign subsidiaries to total subsidiaries (FSUBR) shows the relative importance within the company of its foreign operations. A given company may have extensive foreign operations, yet if it is very large in scale, the relative importance of foreign operations may be less than one might expect.

Ratio of foreign sales to total sales (FSALR) reflects a different mode of conception of the relative importance of foreign operations. A given company may have many domestic subsidiaries that sell a great deal of their output on foreign markets and yet have few actual subsidiaries overseas. Therefore, this ratio in principle measures something quite different from the previous ratio.

Short-run profit orientation (CBO1) requires a bit more explanation. It might be thought that this is a reflection of corporate policy and therefore should be numbered among the dependent variables in the study of corporate policy dimensions. The distinction being made here is between very general corporate policy, which is taken to be analogous to corporate characteristics in size and structure, and specific corporate policies in subsidiary autonomy, performance evaluation, and transfer pricing. The specific policies are determined by the general policy. More precisely, the specific policies depend on a set of factors that includes general policy, corporate characteristics in size and structure, and external environment. It has already been mentioned in section I.B. that in the long run, corporate characteristics are determined by external forces. This point may also be made with respect to general corporate policy. But in the short run, general corporate policy may be considered fixed—or at least one may say that the general policy is far less flexible than specific policies.

The second point concerns the rationale for using only short-run profit orientation out of the list of business objectives. First of all, it must be recognized that the "degrees-of-freedom" problem in statistics operates as a deterrent to adding explanatory variables indiscriminately. The degrees of freedom are the number of observations less the number of coefficients being estimated in a given application. The more degrees of freedom that are present, the stronger are the statistical inferences that one may draw from the data. In particular, the more degrees of freedom that are present, the more likely it is that statistically significant relationships will be gleaned from the data. In efforts to ascertain multiple causation structures with the use of regression analysis or partial correlation analysis, each variable that is added as a potential explanatory variable results in the loss of one degree of freedom. On the other hand, it is of course obvious that one may not delete variables purely on the basis of attempting to achieve a desirable number of degrees of freedom. It is another basic principle of statistical analysis that the deletion of an important explanatory variable may bias and invalidate the results.

The theoretical justification for including short-run profit orientation as the single descriptor of general corporate policy is that it is qualitatively distinct from the other objectives and that it is the best single descriptor of general corporate policy available. It was mentioned above that there is a basic political conflict within any commercial organization between that party concerned with realizing the maximum return within the current or short-term planning period and that party wanting rather to lay a firm foundation for future profits by means of stress on other objectives, such as sales growth, innovation, and so on. This survey has in fact provided some statistical evidence that this political conflict is not purely a theoretical hypothesis but is rather an important part of actual reality. The issue will be discussed further in the next section, but for present purposes it is necessary to refer to Table III.C.6 in the next section, which shows the simple correlation coefficients among various general policy orientations. Notice the fact that short-run profit orientation (CBO1) is inversely related to all but one of the other business objectives and that in most cases this inverse relationship is statistically significant. None of the other objectives shows this extraordinarily uniform inverse relationship among alternative business objectives. On the basis of this evidence as well as the general plausibility of casual empiricism, it is proposed that an emphasis on short-run profit does in fact drastically affect policy formulation in specific areas within the corporation.

One speculation that would account for this is that an emphasis on short-run profit maximization indicates that the corporation is currently in a stressful situation, that the environment has put pressure on the corporation and placed it in a more difficult situation than is typical among large corporations. The emphasis on short-run profit is a manifestation of the motivation within the corporation to restore the situation and move to a more favorable position. In the emphasis on short-run improvement, the future is more or less left to take care of itself, and the other objectives, which are oriented more to the long-term viability and success of the corporation, are correspondingly deemphasized.

The last summary variable is environmental variability (ENVA). This is a general variable representing the overall complexity and stressfulness of the environment as perceived by the upper management of the firm. Again, it might be questioned whether this single variable adequately represents the totality of those factors that are indubitably exogenous in nature, even in the long run. Certainly decomposition of the environmental factors as determinants of policy variables might be instructive. But first of all, there is a limit on what can be presented in a single report. Second, the degrees-of-freedom problem would begin to impinge heavily if the decomposition were made too fine. There was a total of 11 different environmental factors included on the survey questionnaire, and it would be impractical to include each of these as an explanatory factor. Finally, an inspection of the simple-correlation-coefficient matrix among all the environmental factors listed in the questionnaire (shown as Table III.C.8) reveals heavily positive interrelationships among the subjective judgments of importance of the factors to company operations. Of 55 different nontrivial correlations, 24 are significant at the 5 percent level or better, another 5 are significant at the 10 percent-to-5 percent level, and another 8 are significant at the 20 percent-to-10 percent level. All these correlations are positive, as are all but 4 among the 55 different correlations. This suggests that if a given management perceives that unforeseen changes in one environmental factor will have a strong influence on the outcome of subsidiary operations, it will also tend to perceive that unforeseen changes in other factors will have similar influences. This perception of the variability of the environment supports the use of a single variable to represent the environment. Of course this also implies that what is being measured is not the environment itself, but rather the perception of the environment by the management. This is an inevitable consequence of the fact that the study relies on subjective impressions of environmental variability rather than objective measures of it. But within this constraint, a single variable measuring the overall perception of environmental variability in a given corporation will be sufficient.

The seven variables world sales (WSAL), number of subsidiaries (SUB), number of countries (NCOUN), ratio of foreign subsidiaries to total subsidiaries (FSUBR), ratio of foreign sales to total sales (FSALR), short-run profit orientation (CBO1), and environmental variability (ENVA) encompass this study's view of exogenous or independent variables. The objective is to determine the influence of these seven variables on the various specific policy variables, such as profit-oriented performance evaluation (PESMPR) and instrumental transfer pricing (TPMIN). To this end, all summary policy variables shown in Table III.B.1 were stepwise regressed on the seven independent variables listed. Likewise, partial correlations were performed between each variable in the set of summary policy variables and each variable in the set of exogenous variables. Only the latter results will be reported here.

Table III.B.3 is shown to assist in the explanation of this decision. It shows the result of a stepwise regression of usage of instrumental transfer-pricing methods (TPMIN) on the set of seven exogenous variables. The bottom row of the table also shows the result of partial correlation of TPMIN with each of the seven exogenous variables. Instrumental transfer pricing, it will be recalled, refers to the setting of a transfer price on a case-by-case basis, in order to benefit the overall corporation. An important objective of the study is to try to ascertain determinants of a corporation's usage of this type of transfer policy and also the correlates of this type of policy with other policy dimensions.

Stepwise regression is a straightforward extension of standard multiple regression. In standard multiple regression, all the explanatory variables are entered into the equation at once. But in stepwise regression, they are entered one at a time. First, the dependent variable is regressed on each one of the variables in the set of explanatory variables. The variable that best fits (produces the highest R^2) is then selected and entered into the equation. In the second step, the dependent variable is regressed on a series of two-variable combinations. One of the two variables is the variable that was entered on the first step; the other variable is one out of the set of variables that at that point are not yet in the equation. That two-variable combination is selected that has the highest R^2, and so on. One way to envision the procedure is that it constructs the equation in the order that maximizes the rate of increase of R^2. As can well be imagined, the computational demands of the stepwise regression technique are heavy. The reason for the popularity of the technique at the present time is that the development of the modern computer has relegated the computational cost factor to insignificance, except for the most gigantic statistical undertakings.

It may be ascertained from Table III.B.3 that the order of entry of the variables into the equation is as follows: first step—FSUBR (ratio of foreign subsidiaries to total subsidiaries); second step—WSAL (world sales); third step—SUB (number of subsidiaries); fourth step—CBO1 (short-run profit orientation); fifth step—ENVA (environmental variability); sixth step—NCOUN (number of countries

TABLE III.B.3

Stepwise Regression of Usage of Instrumental Pricing on Exogenous
Corporate Characteristics and Environmental Variability
(dependent variable: TPMIN = TPM17—instrumental pricing)

Step	Constant	WSAL	SUB	NCOUN	FSUBR	FSALR	CBO1	ENVA	R^2
				Regression Coefficients of Independent Variables (significance level in parentheses)					
1	.2401				1.0988				.0523
	(.525)				(.110)*				(.110)*
2	.3715	-.2634E-4			1.1866				.0996
	(.382)	(.123)*			(.082)**				(.085)**
3	.2832	-.3738E-4	.3932E-2		1.0305				.1335
	(.505)	(.043)***	(.174)*		(.131)*				(.080)**
4	-.5124	-.3630E-4	.4436E-2		1.0501		.3420		.1664
	(.495)	(.053)**	(.127)*		(.122)*		(.203)*		(.079)**
5	.3787	-.3617E-4	.4401E-2		1.1588		.3265	-.4000	.1788
	(.776)	(.055)**	(.131)*		(.096)**		(.224)	(.420)	(.111)*
6	.3681	-.3138E-4	.5482E-2	-.7723E-2	1.3749		.2922	-.3815	.1847
	(.784)	(.199)*	(.121)*	(.578)	(.088)**		(.292)	(.446)	(.164)*
7	.5237	-.3079E-4	.5784E-2	-.1420E-1	1.1245	1.1786	.2666	-.4652	.1946
	(.702)	(.135)*	(.107)*	(.395)	(.201)*	(.477)	(.343)	(.369)	(.212)

Comparison: Partial Correlation Coefficients with TPMIN (significance level in parentheses)

	WSAL	SUB	NCOUN	FSUBR	FSALR	CBO1	ENVA
	-.2239	.2462	-.1313	.1965	.1099	.1465	-.1387
	(.063)**	(.054)**	(.198)*	(.101)*	(.239)	(.171)*	(.185)*

Code: WSAL   World sales
SUB   Number of subsidiaries
NCOUN   Number of countries
FSUBR   Ratio of foreign subsidiaries to total subsidiaries
FSALR   Ratio of foreign sales to total sales
CBO1   Short-run profit orientation
ENVA   Environmental variability

Note: Sample size is 51 corporations.

in which company operates); seventh step—FSALR (ratio of foreign sales to total sales). The seventh step represents the final equation, with all the explanatory variables entered into it. Immediately below this seventh line is the line of partial correlation coefficients for the corresponding variables.

Two things will be noted in comparing the seventh line of the stepwise multiple regression with the line of partial correlation coefficients. The first is that the signs of the regression coefficients and the partial correlation coefficients are the same. Thus, if multiple regression indicates a positive or negative relationship between TPMIN and one of the exogenous variables, partial correlation will also indicate respectively a positive or negative relationship. The second point is that the significance levels of the partial correlation coefficients are uniformly lower than the significance levels of the corresponding regression coefficients. In fact, several coefficients that are not recognized to be statistically significant using multiple regression are recognized to be such using partial correlation. The result shown in Table III.B.3 was practically universal: regression coefficients had the same signs as partial correlation coefficients but tended to be less significant.

In light of these results, it was decided to forego reporting the results from the multiple regressions. It would seem that little or nothing is lost by so doing. The omitted regression results are almost always in the same direction as the partial correlation results, but statistically they are weaker. There is also the point, as can be seen from Table III.B.3, that to report the full stepwise results would require a great deal of space.

As to why the stepwise regression results are statistically weaker than the partial correlation results, this may well be owing to the existence of multicollinearity among the explanatory variables. As may be verified from inspection of Table III.B.4, there are some strong intercorrelations, mostly of a positive nature, among the set of seven explanatory variables world sales (WSAL), number of subsidiaries (SUB), number of countries in which the company operates (NCOUN), ratio of foreign subsidiaries to total subsidiaries (FSUBR), ratio of foreign sales to total sales (FSALR), short-run profit orientation (CBO1), and environmental variability (ENVA). Multicollinearity is one of the major problems of the multiple regression technique. Strictly speaking, the validity of the approach depends on there being full independence among the set of explanatory variables. That is, none of the explanatory variables should be correlated with another one. Of course, in the vast majority of applications of regression in management science and the social sciences, this condition is nowhere near to being satisfied. The general tendency is to plow ahead with regression anyway, and if the forthcoming results agree with

TABLE III.B.4

Simple Correlation Coefficients among Exogenous Corporate Characteristics and Environmental Variability

	WSAL	SUB	NCOUN	FSUBR	FSALR	CBO1	ENVA
WSAL	1.000						
SUB	.4399 (.001)***	1.000					
NCOUN	.5185 (.001)***	.6636 (.001)***	1.000				
FSUBR	.0836 (.282)	.1875 (.096)**	.4692 (.001)***	1.000			
FSALR	.2654 (.031)***	.3633 (.005)***	.7091 (.001)***	.6226 (.001)***	1.000		
CBO1	-.1102 (.223)	-.1753 (.111)*	-.2701 (.029)***	-.0550 (.352)	-.1007 (.243)	1.000	
ENVA	.0400 (.391)	.0423 (.385)	.1504 (.149)*	.2012 (.081)**	.2926 (.020)***	-.0739 (.305)	1.000

Code: WSAL   World Sales
SUB   Number of subsidiaries
NCOUN Number of countries in which company operates
FSUBR Ratio of foreign subsidiaries to total subsidiaries
FSALR Ratio of foreign sales to total sales
CBO1   Short-run profit orientation
ENVA   Environmental variability

Note: Parentheses indicate significance level. Number of companies in sample is 51.

intuitive and/or theoretical expectations, to assert that apparently the multicollinearity problem did not overcome the tendency in the data to tell the truth. By the same token, if the results run counter to intuition and expectation, multicollinearity is a convenient excuse to be invoked.

The technical effect of the existence of multicollinearity is to increase the standard errors of the regression coefficients, decrease the corresponding t-values, and hence reduce the level of statistical confidence. In short, the significance levels in our parentheses go up, thus reducing the likelihood of being able to specify a given result as statistically significant. Apparently the partial correlation technique evades this problem to a greater extent than the regression technique.

C. Sample Characteristics

The 52 corporations in the sample provide a broad cross-section of large U.S. multinational corporations. The simple correlations reported in this study are based on the full sample of 52 corporations. The partial correlations are based on a sample of 51 corporations. This is because one company out of the 52 did not provide information on foreign sales. Thus, there was not an observation for this company on ratio of foreign sales to total sales (FSALR), which was one of the set of seven key exogenous factors selected for analysis.

Tables III.C.1, III.C.2, III.C.3, and III.C.4 provide information on the scale and structure of the corporations in the sample. The first table shows frequency distributions of world and foreign sales, world and foreign employees, and domestic and foreign subsidiaries. While all these corporations may be classified as large, it is apparent that there is considerable variation among them in scale of operation.

Table III.C.2 shows frequency distributions of percentages indicating the extent of involvement in foreign operations. Again, there is a wide range, from companies that are only marginally involved in foreign operations to those that are heavily involved. A few of the corporations in the sample have overseas commitments that are actually larger than their domestic commitments.

Table III.C.3 shows frequency distributions of percentages indicating the importance of intracompany transfers. Only 39 companies provided a figure for value of imports from foreign subsidiaries to U.S. subsidiaries and only 44 a figure for value of exports from U.S. subsidiaries to foreign subsidiaries. While it would be excessive to say that this represents a poor response rate on these items, the number of missing observations did deter use of one or both of these variables as components of the set of key exogenous variables used in the partial correlation analysis. Again, there is a fairly wide range of percentages, from zero percent to fairly substantial percents in the order of 20 percent or more.

Table III.C.4 shows relative usage of center concepts (investment center, profit center, and cost center) among domestic and foreign subsidiaries. This information is derived from a subsample of 32 companies providing full information on all center queries. The profit center is the most common conception among subsidiaries, followed by investment center, and then cost center. This pattern is the same among domestic and foreign subsidiaries.

Table III.C.5 shows the tabulation of responses to the item class: current business orientation. On the basis of mean response, long-run profit (CBO2) is the leading orientation, followed by new product development (CBO7), growth in sales (CBO3), and increase in market share (CBO4). Short-run profit (CBO1) is tied with technological modernization (CBO8).

Table III.C.6 displays simple correlation coefficients among the various current business objectives. This table gives some insight into the pattern of complementarity and conflict among the various corporate goals. The most striking conflict is between short-run profit (CBO1) and almost every other objective. Notice the generally negative signs of the correlation coefficients in the first column. Most of these negative correlation coefficients are also statistically significant. The one exception to the rule of a negative correlation between short-run profit orientation and other goals is, surprisingly enough, growth in sales (CBO3). Growth in sales is significantly <u>positively</u> associated with short-run profit. This is perhaps not as surprising as it seems on first glance. There is a tendency among business executives to think of unit profit as a constant not affected by the scale of production and sales. If unit profit were indeed constant, an increase in production and sales would of course increase profit. In reality, things are usually not as simple as that: unit profit is likely to be affected by scale of production and sales. However, it is also certainly true that under the appropriate circumstances, an increase in sales will indeed increase profits.

Except for the anomalous result with respect to growth in sales, the other results are as expected. Short-run profit conflicts with all the other goals, while long-run profit is complementary to them. It is interesting to note that even enhanced social responsibility is regarded by the respondents as consistent with long-run profit. The correlation coefficient between long-run profit and enhanced social responsibility is +.2431, which is significant at the 4.1 percent level.

TABLE III.C.1

Frequency Distributions of Variables Indicating Scale of Operation

Variable	Range	Number	Percent
World sales (millions of U.S. dollars)	400–800	11	21
	801–1,200	9	18
	1,201–2,800	11	22
	2,801–4,000	7	13
	4,001–8,000	5	10
	8,001–20,000	4	8
	20,001–60,000	5	10
Foreign sales (millions of U.S. dollars)	30–200	16	31
	201–500	18	38
	501–1,000	2	4
	1,001–1,500	7	13
	1,501–3,000	6	12
	3,001–10,000	4	8
	over 10,000	4	8
	No information	1	2
World employees	under 10,000	10	19
	10,000–20,000	10	19
	20,001–30,000	9	18
	30,001–40,000	5	10
	40,001–50,000	4	8
	50,001–60,000	5	10
	60,001–100,000	5	10
	100,001–200,000	2	4
	200,000–750,000	2	4

	Number	Percent
Foreign employees		
under 10,000	7	14
1,001–3,000	12	23
3,001–5,000	6	12
5,001–10,000	5	10
10,001–20,000	7	13
20,001–30,000	7	13
30,001–100,000	2	4
100,001–230,000	2	4
No information	2	4
Domestic subsidiaries		
0–5	12	22
6–10	8	15
11–15	7	13
16–20	8	15
21–25	5	10
26–30	4	8
31–50	2	4
51–100	4	8
101–120	2	4
Foreign subsidiaries		
0–5	10	19
6–10	7	13
11–15	3	6
16–20	6	12
21–25	5	10
26–30	2	4
31–50	9	17
51–100	5	10
101–250	5	10

Note: Percent is adjusted to nearest whole number. Sample size is 52 corporations.

TABLE III.C.2

Frequency Distributions of Percentage Variables
Indicating Extent of Involvement in Foreign Operations

Variable	Percentage Range	Number	Percent
Foreign sales as a percentage of world sales	1.0 - 10.0	7	14
	10.1 - 20.0	9	18
	20.1 - 30.0	12	24
	30.1 - 40.0	9	18
	40.1 - 50.0	6	12
	50.1 - 60.0	5	10
	60.1 - 65.0	3	6
Total		51	
Foreign employees as a percentage of world employees	0.1 - 10.0	10	20
	10.1 - 20.0	12	24
	20.1 - 30.0	9	18
	30.1 - 40.0	10	20
	40.1 - 50.0	2	4
	50.1 - 60.0	3	6
	60.1 - 75.0	4	8
Total		50	
Foreign subsidiaries as a percentage of total subsidiaries	1.0 - 15.0	4	8
	15.1 - 30.0	5	10
	30.1 - 45.0	8	15
	45.1 - 60.0	6	12
	60.1 - 75.0	15	29
	75.1 - 90.0	11	21
	90.1 - 95.0	3	6
Total		52	

Note: Percent is adjusted to the nearest whole number. Sample size is 52 corporations; however, there was no information from 1 corporation on foreign sales, and no information from 2 corporations on foreign employees.

72

TABLE III.C.3

Frequency Distributions of Percentage Variables
Indicating Importance of Intracompany Transfers

Variable	Percentage Range	Number	Percent
Exports from U.S. sub-sidiaries to foreign subsidiaries as a per-centage of world sales		6	13.6
	.01 – .25	5	11.4
	.26 – .50	4	9.1
	.51 – 1.00	3	6.9
	1.01 – 2.50	4	9.1
	2.51 – 5.00	4	9.1
	5.01 – 7.50	5	11.4
	7.51 – 10.00	5	11.4
	10.01 – 15.00	4	9.1
	15.01 – 19.00	4	9.1
Total		44	
Imports from foreign subsidiaries to U.S. subsidiaries as a per-centage of world sales		16	41.0
	.01 – .25	4	10.2
	.51 – 1.00	6	15.4
	1.01 – 2.50	3	7.7
	2.51 – 5.00	3	7.7
	5.01 – 7.50	2	5.1
	7.51 – 10.00	2	5.1

	18.01 – 27.00	3	7.7
Total		39	

Note: Percent is adjusted to the nearest whole number.
Forty-four companies provided information on value of exports.
Thirty-nine companies provided information on imports.

TABLE III.C.4

Relative Usage of Center Concepts
(mean percent)

	Domestic	Foreign	Total
Investment centers	11.25	9.32	20.58
Profit centers	30.76	34.70	65.46
Cost centers	6.62	7.32	13.95
All centers	48.64	51.35	100.00

Note: Percent is adjusted to the nearest whole number.
Sample size is 32 corporations.

Table III.C.7 is a tabulation of responses to the item class:
environmental factors. The first four factors on the list, government regulations (ENV1), raw material and labor costs (ENV2),
overall demand for commodities produced (ENV3), and level of
competition (ENV4) all happen to have high relative importance
rankings. Table III.C.8 shows a matrix of simple correlation
coefficients among the importance rankings of unforeseen variation in the set of environmental factors ENV1 to ENV11. It will
be noticed that virtually all of these coefficients are positive, and
that a great many of them are statistically significant. It was
argued in the previous section that this indicates that environmental variability is perceived as a totality by the management of a
given corporation, and that this justifies the use of a single measure of overall environmental variability as an exogenous factor
determining (along with other factors involving the scale and structure of corporate operations) specific corporate policies in the
area of subsidiary autonomy, performance evaluation, and transfer pricing.

TABLE III.C.5

Relative Importance of Various Objectives in Current Business Planning
(in percent)

Objective		Very High (3)	High (2)	Low (1)	Very Low (0)	Mean	Standard Deviation
CB01	Short-run profit	31	58	12	0	2.192	.627
CB02	Long-run profit	71	27	2	0	2.692	.506
CB03	Growth in sales	40	48	6	6	2.231	.807
CB04	Increase in market share	35	52	13	0	2.212	.667
CB05	Employment stability	13	62	17	8	1.808	.768
CB06	Employee welfare	17	67	13	2	2.000	.626
CBO7	New product development	63	23	13	0	2.500	.728
CB08	Technological modernization	35	52	12	2	2.192	.715
CB09	Enhanced social responsibility	10	56	27	8	1.673	.760
CBO10	Other	8	2	0	90	.269	.843

Note: Percent is adjusted to the nearest whole number. Sample size is 52 corporations.

TABLE III.C.6

Simple Correlation Coefficients among Current Business Objectives

	CBO1	CBO2	CBO3	CBO4	CBO5	CBO6	CBO7	CBO8	CBO9
CBO1	1.000								
CBO2	-.6124 (.001)***	1.000							
CBO3	.3365 (.007)***	-.1587 (.131)*	1.000						
CBO4	-.0991 (.242)	.1385 (.164)*	.4176 (.001)***	1.000					
CBO5	-.2473 (.039)***	.1978 (.080)**	.1995 (.078)**	.1959 (.082)**	1.000				
CBO6	-.1996 (.078)**	.1855 (.094)**	.1164 (.206)*	.1878 (.091)**	.5708 (.001)***	1.000			
CBO7	-.2148 (.063)**	.1597 (.129)*	.3005 (.015)***	.3840 (.002)***	.1755 (.107)*	.1721 (.111)*	1.000		
CBO8	-.3900 (.002)***	.3291 (.009)***	.1254 (.188)*	.1598 (.129)*	.4614 (.001)***	.3065 (.014)***	.2638 (.029)***	1.000	
CBO9	-.3180 (.011)***	.2431 (.041)***	.1574 (.133)*	.1005 (.239)	.4950 (.001)***	.4945 (.001)***	.4079 (.001)***	.4789 (.001)***	1.000

Code: CBO1 Short-run profit
CBO2 Long-run profit
CBO3 Growth in sales
CBO4 Increased market share
CBO5 Employment stability
CBO6 Employee welfare
CBO7 New product development
CBO8 Technological modernization
CBO9 Enhanced social responsibility

Note: Sample size is 52 corporations.

TABLE III.C.7

Relative Significance of Various Environmental Factors for
Subsidiaries Engaged in International Transfers
(in percent)

Environmental Factor	Highly Significant (3)	Intermediately Significant (2)	Of Little Significance (1)	Mean	Standard Deviation
ENV 1 Government regulations	69	21	10	2.569	.664
ENV 2 Raw material and labor costs	67	33	6	2.558	.608
ENV 3 Overall demand for commodities produced	65	29	6	2.596	.603
ENV 4 Level of competition	58	38	4	2.538	.576
ENV 5 Technological conditions	29	54	17	2.115	.676
ENV 6 Cost of capital (long-term loans)	25	50	25	2.000	.714
ENV 7 Cost of working capital (short-term loans)	21	50	29	1.927	.710
ENV 8 Rates of inflation	44	46	10	2.346	.653
ENV 9 Tax rates	40	48	12	2.288	.667
ENV 10 Exchange rates	38	54	8	2.308	.612
ENV 11 Tariffs, customs duties, import quotas	13	71	15	1.981	.541

Note: Percent is adjusted to the nearest whole number. Sample size is 52 corporations.

77

TABLE III.C.8

Simple Correlation Coefficients among Environmental Factors

	ENV1	ENV2	ENV3	ENV4	ENV5	ENV6	ENV7	ENV8	ENV9	ENV10	ENV11
ENV1	1.000										
ENV2	.2774 (.023)***	1.000									
ENV3	.0254 (.429)	.5201 (.001)***	1.000								
ENV4	.0670 (.319)	.5258 (.001)***	.5238 (.001)***	1.000							
ENV5	.0621 (.331)	.2699 (.026)***	.4536 (.001)***	.2401 (.043)***	1.000						
ENV6	.1240 (.191)*	.0452 (.375)	.2734 (.025)***	.1430 (.156)*	.1625 (.125)*	1.000					
ENV7	.0576 (.343)	.0105 (.471)	.1552 (.136)*	.0074 (.479)	.1415 (.159)*	.7351 (.001)***	1.000				
ENV8	.0122 (.466)	.3439 (.006)***	.2126 (.065)**	.3286 (.009)***	.2630 (.030)***	.2522 (.001)***	.4391 (.001)***	1.000			
ENV9	.4451 (.001)***	.0307 (.414)	.1980 (.080)**	.2003 (.077)**	.0552 (.349)	.2883 (.019)***	.3793 (.003)***	.3064 (.014)***	1.000		
ENV10	.1670 (.118)*	.2151 (.063)**	.0778 (.292)	.1327 (.174)*	.0073 (.480)	.3143 (.012)***	.4621 (.001)***	.6115 (.001)***	.4512 (.001)***	1.000	
ENV11	.1958 (.082)**	-.0859 (.272)	.0358 (.401)	-.0290 (.419)	-.1009 (.238)	.1520 (.141)*	.0980 (.245)	-.0362 (.399)	.2870 (.020)***	.3140 (.012)***	1.000

Code: ENV1 Government regulations
ENV2 Raw material and labor costs
ENV3 Overall demand for commodities
ENV4 Level of competition
ENV5 Technological conditions
ENV6 Cost of capital (long-term loans)

ENV 7 Cost of working capital (short-term loans)
ENV 8 Rates of inflation
ENV 9 Tax rates
ENV 10 Exchange rates
ENV 11 Tariffs, customs duties, import quotas

Note: Parentheses indicate significance level. Sample size is 52 corporations.

NOTES

1. Seung L. Kim and Stephen L. Miller, "Constituents of the International Transfer-Pricing Decision," Columbia Journal of World Business 14 (Spring 1979):69-77.

2. Roger Y. W. Tang, Transfer-Pricing Practices in the U.S. and Japan (New York: Praeger, 1979).

3. Robert K. Mautz, Financial Reporting by Diversified Companies (New York: Financial Executives Research Foundation, 1968).

4. James H. Greene and Michael G. Duerr, Intercompany Transactions in the Multinational Firm (New York: The Conference Board, 1970).

5. Ralph L. Benke, Jr. and James Don Edwards, Transfer Pricing: Techniques and Uses (New York: National Association of Accountants, 1980).

6. Two examples of utilization of numerical scoring of relative-importance judgments to be found in the accounting survey literature on transfer pricing are Kim and Miller and Tang, cited above respectively in notes 1 and 2.

Questionnaire Mailing Packet

Contents

1. Cover letter

2. Questionnaire form

3. Project description

4. Follow-up cover letter

5. Selected information in

    follow-up mailing

Note: The questionnaires on the following pages have been greatly reduced in scale in order to conform to margin requirements.

COVER LETTER

The rapidly accumulating theoretical literature on transfer pricing and performance evaluation in multinational corporations suffers from a serious deficiency. It is not based on a sufficient amount of empirical evidence concerning actual practices in the real world.

The purpose of my survey study is to help fill in some of the gaps in the empirical evidence. It would help both me and all those interested in business policy if you, or someone on your staff, would set aside half an hour to complete the enclosed questionnaire and return it to me in the postpaid envelope provided.

I absolutely guarantee the confidentiality of your response. To preserve anonymity, if desired, it is only necessary to omit the name and address of your corporation on the questionnaire form. The purpose of this survey is to generate aggregate statistics, and when these statistics have been obtained, the individual responses will be discarded.

Some of the questions require fairly subtle judgments on the relative importances of various characteristics, criteria, methods, objectives, and so forth. It is recognized that the answers given by any particular respondent may be quite subjective and impressionistic. Please be assured that a response based on informed intuition is infinitely more valuable than no response at all. Very often statistically reliable information can be obtained from responses which seem to the individual respondents to be little more than "hunches" or "guesswork."

A copy of the summary results from this survey, when it is completed, will be provided to any responding company requesting it.

Thanking you in advance for your attention to this inquiry,
I am,

Sincerely yours,

Penelope J. Yunker
Assistant Professor of Accounting

Enclosures: 4 page questionnaire
postpaid return envelope
project description
sponsor information

PROJECT: Transfer Pricing and
Performance Evaluation in
Multinational Corporations

SPONSOR: Center for Business and Economic Research
College of Business
Western Illinois University
Prof. Richard Hattwick, Director

DIRECTOR: Prof. Elwood Miller
Department of Accounting
St. Louis University

ASSOCIATE: Prof. Penelope Yunker
Department of Accountancy
College of Business
Western Illinois University

QUESTIONNAIRE ON TRANSFER PRICING AND PERFORMANCE EVALUATION
IN MULTINATIONAL CORPORATIONS

To the Respondent: *Thank you for your consideration in filling out this form.*

All responses are considered strictly confidential: the completed forms will be destroyed after general statistics are obtained.

If you desire a summary of the report based on this survey, check the box below:

☐ *PLEASE SEND A SUMMARY REPORT*
(if checked, identify company below)

Person completing form (optional):

Name and Position: _____

A. Company Characteristics

(Please give estimates if exact figures are unknown or difficult to ascertain.)

Name of Company (optional): _____

Headquarters Address (optional): _____

82

Number of employees worldwide: _____

Number of employees outside U.S.: _____

Sales worldwide (U.S. dollars): _____

Sales outside U.S. (U.S. dollars): _____

Value of exports from U.S. subsidiaries
to foreign subsidiaries (U.S. dollars): _____

Value of imports from foreign subsidiaries
to U.S. subsidiaries (U.S. collars): _____

Number of chiefly manufacturing subsidiaries:

Domestic: _____   Foreign: _____

Number of chiefly marketing subsidiaries:

Domestic: _____   Foreign: _____

Number of domestic subsidiaries: _____

Number of foreign subsidiaries: _____

Number of countries in which
foreign subsidiaries are located: _____

Number of investment center subsidiaries:

Domestic: _____   Foreign: _____

Number of profit center subsidiaries:

Domestic: _____   Foreign: _____

Number of cost center subsidiaries:

Domestic: _____   Foreign: _____

Current Business Orientation: From the point of view of the overall corporation, relatively how important are the following objectives in your current business planning? (please check the best response -- one check in each line)

Objective	Degree of Importance			
	Very High	High	Low	Very Low
Short run profit				
Long run profit				
Growth in sales				
Increase in market share				
Employment stability				
Employee welfare				
New product development				
Technological modernization				
Enhanced social responsibility				
Other (please specify):				

B. Transfer Pricing for International Transactions

1. General Objectives: From the point of view of the overall corporation, relatively how important are the following objectives in your international transfer pricing system?

General Objective	Dominant Objective	Very Important Objective	Somewhat Important Objective	Not Important
Simplicity and ease of application				
Facilitate performance evaluation of managers				
Increase overall corporate profit				
Increase overall corporate sales				
Other (please specify):				

2. General Policy: From the point of view of the overall corporation, relatively how often are the following specific transfer pricing methods utilized for international transfers?

Method	Always Used	Often Used	Sometimes Used	Rarely Used	Never Used
Actual unit variable cost					
Actual unit full cost					
Standard unit variable cost					
Standard unit full cost					
Actual unit variable cost plus fixed markup					
Actual unit full cost plus fixed markup					
Standard unit variable cost plus fixed markup					
Standard unit full cost plus fixed markup					
Marginal cost (incremental cost)					
Opportunity cost					
Dual pricing					
Mathematical programming optimal price					
Market price					
Adjusted market price (market price less selling costs)					
Negotiated price (unit cost plus negotiated markup)					
Contribution margin					

Instrumental price* (see below for definition)						
No transfer price (free transfers)						
Ad hoc transfer price (not based on general policy)						
Other (please specify):						

3. *Instrumental prices -- specific objective prices. Instrumental pricing refers to the setting of a transfer price markup or a transfer price itself by the parent company on a case-by-case basis to benefit the overall corporation.

From the point of view of the overall corporation, in those cases when transfer prices are used for instrumental purposes, relatively how important are the following specific objectives in your international transfer pricing system?

Specific Objective	Degree of Importance			
	High	Medium	Low	None
Take advantage of economies of scale in production				
Provide inexpensive materials for importing subsidiaries				
Stabilize the competitive position of a subsidiary				
Maintain good relations with host countries				
Reduce currency fluctuation losses				
Reduce customs duty payments				
Reduce sales tax payments				
Reduce corporate profits or income taxes				
Avoid restrictions or earnings repatriation				
Other (please specify):				

85

C. Performance Evaluation

1. Criteria: From the point of view of the overall corporation, relatively how important are the following general principles and specific measures in the performance evaluation of managers of foreign and domestic subsidiaries engaged in <u>international transfers</u>?

	Very Important	Of Some Importance	Of Minor Importance	Of No Importance
General Principles				
Financial measures expressed in U.S. dollars				
Financial measures expressed in local currency				
Standards set by company-wide performance				
Standards set by industry-wide performance				
Standards set by economy-wide performance				
Standards tailored to specific circumstances				
Other (please specify):				
Specific Measures				
Ratio of profits to equity				
Ratio of profits to total assets				
Ratio of profits to sales				
Remittances to parent company				
Net income (profits)				
Residual income (profits after capital charge)				
Sales growth				
Market share				
Cost reduction				
Adherence to budgets				
Meeting plan goals				
Production technological innovation				
New product innovation				
Other (please specify):				

2. Instruments: From the point of view of the overall corporation, relatively how independent are the managers of foreign and domestic subsidiaries engaged in international transfers with respect to each of the following business policy variables?

Instrument	Subsidiary determines entirely	Subsidiary determines mostly	Parent determines mostly	Parent determines entirely
Physical quantities produced				
Price on sales to subsidiaries in same country				
Price on sales to subsidiaries in other countries				
Price on sales outside company				
Quantity of items sold to other subsidiaries				
Quantity of items purchased from other subsidiaries				
Materials and labor purchased in open market				
Major capital investments				
Dividends remitted to parent company				
Major borrowings				
Marketing expenditures				
Research and development expenditures				
Other (please specify):				

3. Environment: From the point of view of the overall corporation, how significant are the effects of unforeseen changes in the following environmental factors on the results of the operations of foreign and domestic subsidiaries engaged in international transfers?

Environmental Factor	Highly Significant	Intermediately Significant	Of Little Significance
Government regulations			
Raw material and labor costs			
Overall demand for commodities produced			
Level of competition			
Technological conditions			
Cost of capital (long-term loans)			
Cost of working capital (short-term loans)			
Rates of inflation			
Tax rates			
Exchange rates			
Tariffs, customs duties, import quotas			
Other (please specify):			

THIS SECTION IS OPTIONAL

D. Specific Thoughts and Concerns

The respondent is urged to write down any thoughts or special knowledge he or she may have on the relationships between transfer pricing and performance evaluation in multinational companies. Such voluntary contributions will materially assist in the interpretation of the results obtained from this survey. Specific topics that could be addressed include--but are not confined to--the following:

--Problems in setting subsidiary goals to enhance corporate goals

--Problems in revising transfer pricing methods

--Potential conflicts between transfer pricing objectives and performance evaluation methods

--Specific issues and conflicts relating to these problems in your own company

--Successful problem resolutions in your own company

(Please append extra sheets if needed.)

RETURN TO: P. J. Yunker
Department of Accounting
Western Illinois University
Macomb, Illinois 61455

PROJECT DESCRIPTION

Transfer Pricing and Performance Evaluation
in Multinational Corporations

TOPIC: Potential conflicts in business enterprises between transfer-pricing objectives and performance-
evaluation objectives have been intensively discussed
in the business policy literature. The best known
problem concerns the possibility of "artificial" variations in the profitability of various subsidiaries owing to a particular transfer pricing system designed
to benefit the corporation as a whole. Such a system may appreciably complicate performance evaluation of the managers of the various subsidiaries
engaged in intra-company transfers. The potential
conflicts between transfer-pricing objectives and
performance-evaluation objectives, which are already
substantial in the case of domestic transfers, become
even more aggravated in the case of international
transfers between subsidiaries of multinational enterprises because of the greater complexity of the
international business environment.

Most of the contributions in the business policy
literature concerning this issue have been in the
nature of "theoretical recommendations." The various authors are usually concerned with developing
recommendations for appropriate transfer-pricing
methods given various circumstances in the business
environment. A common criticism of this approach
is that unrealistically restrictive conditions must
ordinarily be assumed in order to show that the specific recommended policy is optimal.

The study of this particular business policy problem has reached the point where considerable benefit
would be realized from an empirical investigation of
actual practices in the real world. The survey
planned for this project is unprecedented in that it
will collect information both on transfer-pricing
policies and performance-evaluation policies. It is
anticipated that this information will enable us to

89

establish, at least in broad outline, the major patterns of accommodation between transfer pricing and performance evaluation in the actual business environment. These patterns may then be compared with the recommended patterns in the theoretical literature as a means of more effectively channeling prescriptive efforts in the future.

SPONSOR: The Center for Business and Economic Research of Western Illinois University is active in a wide range of projects designed to enhance both academic and public understanding and appreciation of the role of business enterprise in both national and international society. Among the efforts of the Center are included: 1) support of research by College of Business faculty with funds provided by Western Illinois University, by private business corporations and non-profit associations, and by state and national funding agencies; 2) coordination of the Illinois Business Hall of Fame and the American National Business Hall of Fame; 3) editing and publishing the interdisciplinary scholarly periodical The Journal of Behavioral Economics.

DIRECTOR: Dr. Elwood Miller of the Department of Accounting at Saint Louis University is a recognized authority on multinational enterprise. He has published two recent books: Accounting Problems of Multinational Enterprises (Lexington, 1979), and Inflation Accounting (Van Nostrand Reinhold, 1980); as well as several articles in professional periodicals including the Harvard Business Review.

ASSOCIATE: Penelope Yunker (M.A., C.P.A.) is an Assistant Professor of Accountancy at Western Illinois University, and a Ph.D. candidate at Saint Louis University. This survey is part of her dissertation research.

90

FOLLOW-UP LETTER

In December I sent a questionnaire on transfer pricing and performance evaluation to a large number of corporations with operations abroad. Thus far some 51 corporations have responded. I enclose a copy of the survey form with the percentage of respondents selecting each answer in the hope that you may find some of the information interesting.

In the event that you have not, for one reason or another, returned the questionnaire, I am enclosing a second copy of it, along with a self-addressed, postpaid envelope. I would be very much obliged if you would have some member of your staff, or other knowledgeable person in the company, fill out the questionnaire in all or in part, and return it to me.

We are particularly interested in developing statistical relationships between transfer pricing policies and performance evaluation policies in multinational companies. The more observations we have, the greater will be the degree of reliability of the statistical relationships obtained. Ultimately the purpose of this research is to assist management in achieving higher levels of efficiency and productivity as a means of benefiting the entire society.

Thanking you in advance for your assistance on this project, I remain,

Sincerely yours,

Penelope J. Yunker
Assistant Professor

PROJECT: Transfer Pricing and
          Performance Evaluation in
          Multinational Corporations

DIRECTOR: Prof. Elwood Miller
           Department of Accounting
           St. Louis University

SPONSOR: Center for Business and Economic Research
          College of Business
          Western Illinois University
          Prof. Richard Hattwick, Director

ASSOCIATE: Prof. Penelope Yunker
            Department of Accountancy
            College of Business
            Western Illinois University

QUESTIONNAIRE ON TRANSFER PRICING AND PERFORMANCE EVALUATION
IN MULTINATIONAL CORPORATIONS

To the Respondent: *Thank you for your consideration in filling out this form.*

All responses are considered strictly confidential: the completed forms will be destroyed after general statistics are obtained.

If you desire a summary of the report based on this survey, check the box below:

☐

PLEASE SEND A SUMMARY REPORT
(if checked, identify company below)

Person completing form (optional):

Name and Position: _____

A. Company Characteristics
    (Please give estimates if exact figures are unknown or difficult to ascertain.)

Name of Company (optional): _____

Headquarters Address (optional): _____

92

Number of employees worldwide: _____

Number of employees outside U.S.: _____

Sales worldwide (U.S. dollars): _____

Sales outside U.S. (U.S. dollars): _____

Value of exports from U.S. subsidiaries
to foreign subsidiaries (U.S. dollars): _____

Value of imports from foreign subsidiaries
to U.S. subsidiaries (U.S. dollars): _____

Number of chiefly manufacturing subsidiaries:

Domestic: _____   Foreign: _____

Number of chiefly marketing subsidiaries:

Domestic: _____   Foreign: _____

Number of domestic subsidiaries: _____

Number of foreign subsidiaries: _____

Number of countries in which
foreign subsidiaries are located: _____

Number of investment center subsidiaries:

Domestic: _____   Foreign: _____

Number of profit center subsidiaries:

Domestic: _____   Foreign: _____

Number of cost center subsidiaries:

Domestic: _____   Foreign: _____

Current Business Orientation: From the point of view of the overall corporation, relatively how important
are the following objectives in your current business planning?
(please check the best response -- one check in each line)

Objective	Degree of Importance			
	Very High	High	Low	Very Low
Short run profit	32.3	58.1	9.7	0
Long run profit	71.0	29.0	0	0
Growth in sales	71.0	29.0	6.5	9.7
Increase in market share	38.7	45.2	6.5	0
Employment stability	29.0	54.8	16.1	3.2
Employee welfare	12.9	67.7	16.1	0
New product development	54.8	29.0	16.1	3.2
Technological modernization	35.5	45.2	16.1	3.2
Enhanced social responsibility	3.2	61.3	29.0	6.5
Other (please specify):				

93

B. Transfer Pricing for International Transactions

1. General Objectives: From the point of view of the overall corporation, relatively how important are the following objectives in your international transfer pricing system?

General Objective	Dominant Objective	Very Important Objective	Somewhat Important Objective	Not Important
Simplicity and ease of application	3.2	54.8	38.7	3.2
Facilitate performance evaluation of managers	6.5	29.0	45.2	19.3
Increase overall corporate profit	45.2	25.8	16.1	12.9
Increase overall corporate sales	6.5	25.8	22.6	45.2
Other (please specify):				

2. General Policy: From the point of view of the overall corporation, relatively how often are the following specific transfer pricing methods utilized for international transfers?

Method	Always Used	Often Used	Sometimes Used	Rarely Used	Never Used
Actual unit variable cost	0	3.2	9.7	19.3	67.7
Actual unit full cost	0	9.7	6.5	16.1	67.7
Standard unit variable cost	0	3.2	6.5	22.6	67.7
Standard unit full cost	6.5	6.5	16.1	19.3	51.6
Actual unit variable cost plus fixed markup	0	3.2	12.9	19.3	64.5
Actual unit full cost plus fixed markup	3.2	12.9	19.3	9.7	54.8
Standard unit variable cost plus fixed markup	0	0	6.5	22.6	67.7
Standard unit full cost plus fixed markup	12.9	29.0	9.7	18.1	32.3
Marginal cost (incremental cost)	0	0	3.2	29.0	67.7
Opportunity cost	0	0	0	22.6	77.4
Dual pricing	3.2	0	0	19.3	77.4
Mathematical programming optimal price	0	0	0	9.7	90.3
Market price	12.9	29.0	19.3	12.9	25.8
Adjusted market price (market price less selling costs)	9.7	25.8	12.9	9.7	41.9
Negotiated price (unit cost plus negotiated markup)	3.2	16.1	29.0	6.5	45.2
Contribution margin	0	3.2	0	19.3	77.4

	9.7	9.7	12.9	22.6	45.2
Instrumental price* (see below for definition)					
No transfer price (free transfers)	0	3.2	6.5	6.5	83.9
Ad hoc transfer price (not based on general policy)	0	9.7	6.5	9.7	74.2
Other (please specify):					

*Instrumental prices -- specific objective prices. Instrumental pricing refers to the setting of a transfer price markup or a transfer price itself by the parent company on a case-by-case basis to benefit the overall corporation.

3. From the point of view of the overall corporation, in those cases when transfer prices are used for instrumental purposes, relatively how important are the following specific objectives in your international transfer pricing system?

Specific Objective	Degree of Importance			
	High	Medium	Low	None
Take advantage of economies of scale in production	12.9	16.1	12.9	58.1
Provide inexpensive materials for importing subsidiaries	19.3	3.2	12.9	64.5
Stabilize the competitive position of a subsidiary	9.7	22.6	16.1	51.6
Maintain good relations with host countries	16.1	16.1	19.3	48.4
Reduce currency fluctuation losses	6.5	16.1	22.6	54.8
Reduce customs duty payments	9.7	16.1	19.3	54.8
Reduce sales tax payments	6.5	6.5	25.8	61.3
Reduce corporate profits or income taxes	16.1	19.3	6.5	58.1
Avoid restrictions on earnings repatriation	19.3	12.9	12.9	54.8
Other (please specify):				

PLEASE CHECK THE BEST RESPONSE

C. Performance Evaluation

1. Criteria: From the point of view of the overall corporation, relatively how important are the following general principles and specific measures in the performance evaluation of managers of foreign and domestic subsidiaries engaged in international transfers?

	Very Important	Of Some Importance	Of Minor Importance	Of No Importance
General Principles				
Financial measures expressed in U.S. dollars	58.1	29.0	9.7	3.2
Financial measures expressed in local currency	41.9	35.5	22.6	0
Standards set by company-wide performance	38.7	35.5	6.5	19.3
Standards set by industry-wide performance	6.5	51.6	16.1	25.8
Standards set by economy-wide performance	6.5	41.9	38.7	12.9
Standards tailored to specific circumstances	22.6	45.2	29.0	3.2
Other (Please specify):				
Specific Measures				
Ratio of profits to equity	35.5	25.8	22.6	16.1
Ratio of profits to total assets	51.6	29.0	12.9	6.5
Ratio of profits to sales	45.2	38.7	12.9	3.2
Remittances to parent company	6.5	45.8	45.2	22.6
Net income (profits)	54.8	32.3	3.2	9.7
Residual income (profits after capital charge)	22.6	22.6	29.0	25.8
Sales growth	54.8	29.0	9.7	6.5
Market share	41.9	41.9	9.7	6.5
Cost reduction	51.6	41.9	6.5	0
Adherence to budgets	67.7	25.8	3.2	3.2
Meeting plan goals	67.7	32.3	0	0
Production technological innovation	22.6	51.6	16.1	9.7
New product innovation	22.6	51.6	12.9	12.9
Other (please specify):				

2. Instruments: From the point of view of the overall corporation, relatively how independent are the managers of foreign and domestic subsidiaries engaged in international transfers with respect to each of the following business policy variables?

Instrument	Subsidiary determines entirely	Subsidiary determines mostly	Parent determines mostly	Parent determines entirely	
Physical quantities produced	41.9	25.8	22.6	3.2	6.5
Price on sales to subsidiaries in same country	32.3	32.3	6.5	12.9	16.1
Price on sales to subsidiaries in other countries	25.8	22.6	32.3	12.9	6.5
Price on sales outside company	45.2	38.7	9.7	3.2	3.2
Quantity of items sold to other subsidiaries	25.8	32.3	29.0	6.5	6.5
Quantity of items purchased from other subsidiaries	25.8	35.5	29.0	3.2	6.5
Materials and labor purchased in open market	32.3	64.5	0	0	3.2
Major capital investments	0	9.7	61.3	29.0	0
Dividends remitted to parent company	0	12.9	35.5	51.6	0
Major borrowings	0	12.9	32.3	54.8	0
Marketing expenditures	16.1	61.3	9.7	12.9	0
Research and development expenditures	6.5	35.5	29.0	25.8	3.2
Other (please specify):					

3. Environment: From the point of view of the overall corporation, how significant are the effects of unforeseen changes in the following environmental factors on the results of the operations of foreign and domestic subsidiaries engaged in international transfers?

Environmental Factor	Highly Significant	Intermediately Significant	Of Little Significance
Government regulations	74.2	22.6	3.2
Raw material and labor costs	64.5	29.0	6.5
Overall demand for commodities produced	58.1	35.5	6.5
Level of competition	61.3	38.7	0
Technological conditions	29.0	51.6	19.3
Cost of capital (long-term loans)	29.0	48.4	22.6
Cost of working capital (short-term loans)	22.6	48.4	29.0
Rates of inflation	41.9	48.4	9.7
Tax rates	45.2	45.2	9.7
Exchange rates	38.7	54.8	6.5
Tariffs, customs duties, import quotas	16.1	67.7	16.1
Other (please specify):			

4

ANALYSIS
OF SURVEY
RESULTS

A. Findings on Autonomy

Table IV.A.1 is a tabulation of responses to the instrument
items. It is apparent that the subsidiaries have the greatest amount
of freedom with respect to short-run operations not directly con-
nected with other subsidiaries. The highest independence ratings
are for the instruments physical quantities produced (INST1), price
on sales outside company (INST4), and materials and labor purchased in the open market (INST7).

As would be expected, there is less autonomy with respect to
activities directly affecting other subsidiaries, which are covered
by price on sales to subsidiaries in same country (INST2), price
on sales to subsidiaries in other countries (INST3), quantity of
items sold to other subsidiaries (INST5), and quantity of items purchased from other subsidiaries (INST6). Within this category,
there is about the same amount of freedom for all except price on
sales to subsidiaries in other countries (INST3), which has a dis-
tinctly lower independence rating. Since the dividing line showing
an equal division of authority between the subsidiary company and
the parent company would be a mean response of 2.50 (halfway between "subsidiary determines mostly" and "parent determines
mostly"), it can be said that price on sales to subsidiaries in same
country (INST2), quantity of items sold to other subsidiaries (INST5),
and quantity of items purchased from other subsidiaries (INST6)
fall well on the subsidiary-control side of the line, while price on
sales to subsidiaries in other countries (INST3) falls right on the
line. It is significant that there is more control on price of international intracompany transfers than on domestic transfers. This

TABLE IV.A.1

Autonomy of Managers of Subsidiaries Engaged in International Transfers
with Respect to Various Business-Policy Instruments

(in percent)

Instrument	Subsidiary Determines Entirely (4)	Subsidiary Determines Mostly (3)	Parent Determines Mostly (2)	Parent Determines Entirely (1)	Mean	Standard Deviation
INST1 Physical quantities produced	40	31	23	6	3.058	.938
INST2 Price on sales to subsidiaries in same country	29	42	15	13	2.865	.991
INST3 Price on sales to subsidiaries in other countries	19	29	37	15	2.519	.980
INST4 Price on sales outside company	38	50	8	4	3.231	.757
INST5 Quantity of items sold to other subsidiaries	27	40	23	10	2.846	.937
INST6 Quantity of items purchased from other subsidiaries	27	42	27	4	2.923	.837
INST7 Materials and labor purchased in the open market	35	60	4	2	3.269	.630
INST8 Major capital investments	0	10	56	35	1.750	.622
INST9 Dividends remitted to parent company	0	12	37	52	1.596	.693
INST10 Major borrowings	0	10	42	48	1.615	.661
INST11 Marketing expenditures	13	60	17	10	2.769	.807
INST12 Research and development expenditures	4	31	35	29	2.098	.878

Note: Percent is adjusted to nearest whole number. Sample size is 52 corporations.

is confirmation of the greater importance of instrumental transfer pricing in international transfers than in domestic transfers.

The lower level of autonomy with respect to variables directly affecting the performance of other subsidiaries is, of course, inherent in the centralization of authority within the corporation. It is axiomatic that what is best for the individual subsidiary is not necessarily best for the overall corporation. If a corporation wishes to concentrate profits in subsidiary A because it is operating in a lower-tax area and specifies transfer prices with respect to subsidiaries B, C, and D accordingly, subsidiaries B, C, and D are likely to require a certain amount of coercion to accept these transfer prices. The fact that these variables have a lower independence rating than external instruments is merely evidence that some amount of coordination is imposed from the center in diversified companies. What is perhaps surprising is not that the independence ratings on internal-dealing instruments are lower than those for external-dealing instruments, but that they are not lower than found here. Note, for example, that the subsidiary firms have a great deal more latitude with respect to prices and quantities involved in intracompany transfers than they do with respect to major capital investments (INST8).

The least amount of autonomy is in the category of long-term business instruments such as major capital investments (INST8), major borrowings (INST9), and research and development expenditures (INST12). These results are in line with the result reported above that over 65 percent of the subsidiaries of the respondent companies are considered as profit centers rather than investment centers (Table III.C.4). The head office of the corporation is more likely to take a strong hand in the determination of these policy variables because of their long-run significance to the overall corporation and because, unlike the short-term decision variables such as quantities produced and prices, their effective determination does not require a great deal of specific, short-term information about the conditions prevailing in the local markets of the various subsidiaries.

Table IV.A.2 shows uniformly high positive correlations among the various summary variables pertaining to subsidiary-autonomy policy. For example, a high autonomy level with respect to short-term instruments will tend to be associated with a high autonomy level with respect to long-term instruments as well. This indicates that autonomy policy is uniform within the corporation and is not determined separately for each category of instrument. The correlation between the two alternative measures of short-run instrument (INSTSR1 and INSTSR2) is very close. The only difference between the two measures is that the second one includes marketing expenditures while the first one does not. There was some question as to whether marketing expenditures were better regarded as a short-run instrument or a long-run instrument. The correlation between the two measures is so tight, however, that hereafter only one measure of short-run-instrument autonomy will be used. This will be the second measure that does include marketing expenditures as a short-run instrument.

TABLE IV.A.2

Simple Correlation Coefficients among Summary
Variables Relating to Subsidiary Autonomy

	INSTA	INSTSR1	INSTSR2	INSTLR	INSTIN
INSTA	1.000				
INSTSR1	.8506	1.000			
	(.001)***				
INSTSR2	.8586	.9827	1.000		
	(.001)***	(.001)***			
INSTLR	.7288	.4980	.5468	1.000	
	(.001)***	(.001)***	(.001)***		
INSTIN	.8713	.6451	.6098	.4250	1.000
	(.001)***	(.001)***	(.001)***	(.001)***	

Code: INSTA   Average autonomy, all instruments
      INSTSR1 Average autonomy, short-run instruments
               (first measure)
      INSTSR2 Average autonomy, short run instruments
               (second measure)
      INSTLR   Average autonomy, long-run instruments
      INSTIN   Average autonomy, internal instruments
Note: Parentheses indicate significance level. Sample size is
52 corporations.

Table IV.A.3 shows partial correlation coefficients among the various summary variables on subsidiary autonomy and the seven key exogenous variables selected for analysis. The results are not as good, in terms of statistical significance, as are some of the other results reported in other sections of this chapter. However, some indications are worthy of mention. The financial scale of the organization as measured by world sales (WSAL) has a positive

TABLE IV.A.3

Partial Correlation Coefficients among Summary Variables Pertaining to Subsidiary Autonomy Policy and Exogenous Corporate Characteristics and Environmental Variability

	WSAL	SUB	NCOUN	FSUBR	FSALR	CBO1	ENVA
INSTA	.1974	.0849	-.1392	-.0680	.0979	-.1200	.1640
	(.097)***	(.290)	(.181)*	(.329)	(.261)	(.216)	(.141)*
INSTSR	.0525	.0056	-.0108	.0570	.0057	-.0874	.1595
	(.366)	(.486)	(.472)	(.355)	(.485)	(.284)	(.148)*
INSTLR	.1677	-.0160	.0123	.0393	.0804	-.1101	.0801
	(.135)*	(.465)	(.468)	(.399)	(.300)	(.236)	(.300)
INSTIN	.2253	.1810	-.3048	-.1981	.1499	-.1278	.1618
	(.068)**	(.117)*	(.021)***	(.069)**	(.163)*	(.201)*	(.144)*

Code:
INSTA   All instruments
INSTSR   Short-run instruments
INSTLR   Long-run instruments
INSTIN   Internal transaction instruments
WSAL   World sales
SUB   Number of subsidiaries
NCOUN   Number of countries in which company operates
FSUBR   Ratio of foreign subsidiaries to total subsidiaries
FSALR   Ratio of foreign sales to total sales
CBO1   Short-run profit orientation
ENVA   Environmental variability

Note: Parentheses indicate significance level. See page 56 for explication of asterisk use. Sample size is 51 corporations.

effect on subsidiary autonomy in long-run instruments, internal instruments, and overall instruments. This seems natural, in that efforts at coordination of activity become more difficult as the size and complexity of the organization become very large. Perceived environmental complexity (ENVA) also seems generally positively associated with autonomy, although the effect is weaker. This also makes sense: if the parent company believes the external environment to be extremely complex, it might be more inclined to leave responsibility to the local managers, who have the best knowledge of local conditions. It should also be noted that short-run profit orientation (CBO1) is negatively related to all measures of instrumental autonomy, and in each case the significance level approaches the critical 20 percent level necessary for making a judgment that a relationship exists in fact. A conflict between short-run profit orientation and subsidiary autonomy certainly seems plausible, which inclines us toward accepting this result as statistically significant.

It has been argued by several authors that there are more opportunities for profitable coordination of subsidiary activity in the international business environment than in the domestic environment. Indeed, Miller writes "Decentralization is the antithesis of multinational enterprise" and that the "size and flexibility of an MNC are effective assets only because they can be manipulated in the best interest of the total organization in the long run."[1] As was noted, size per se, without regard to whether the firm is operating domestically or internationally, is positively related to autonomy and decentralization. At the same time, there is a positive correlation between size and international involvement (see Table III.B.4). The hypothesis of Miller and other writers is, however, that as the extent of involvement in international operations of a firm of given size increases, there should be a decline in autonomy. Table IV.A.3 offers partial verification of this hypothesis. Autonomy with respect to internal dealing instruments (INSTIN) is inversely affected by two measures of international involvement: number of countries in which a company operates (NCOUN) and ratio of foreign subsidiaries to total subsidiaries (FSUBR). The strong effects of these variables are what is responsible for the inverse effect of NCOUN on overall subsidiary autonomy (INSTA). This result is consistent with the expectations generated by the previous discussion of the literature on transfer pricing. There are more opportunities for instrumental transfer pricing in the international context, and as instrumental transfer pricing tends to involve one subsidiary gaining at the expense of another, it is natural that more coercion should be necessary when instrumental transfer pricing is used to a great extent.

On the other hand, there is no indication that as international involvement increases there is a decline in the autonomy that subsidiaries are granted with respect to business instrument variables not directly related to intracompany transfers. In fact, the effect of the foreign-sales ratio (FSALR) on internal dealing autonomy is positive and statistically significant by the standard adopted. It is true, on the other hand, that the foreign-sales ratio is not as good an indication of foreign involvement as is the foreign-subsidiary ratio, since many sales are made by domestic subsidiaries to final customers abroad and the interaction in this is limited.

B. Findings on Performance Evaluation

The tabulation of the responses to the items on performance evaluation, general principles and performance evaluation, specific measures is shown in Table IV.B.1. Some of the inferences to be drawn from this table are discussed below.

First, financial measures as expressed in U.S. dollars or in terms of local currency are both important in performance evaluation, but the former is considerably more important than the latter. The question of dollar measures versus local-currency measures has become much more important over the past ten years than it was before then. When exchange rates were relatively constant over time, it made little difference whether performance was evaluated in dollars or in local currency. But under circumstances in which the currency unit of a country in which a subsidiary is operating is appreciating relative to the dollar, the performance of the subsidiary in dollar terms will look much better than the performance of another subsidiary doing the same as the first in terms of local currency but whose local currency is deteriorating in terms of the dollar. The influence of currency value fluctuations must be eliminated from manager evaluations, although they may be very relevant to subsidiary evaluation. Even with respect to subsidiary evaluation, it is questionable whether long-term investment, acquisition, or devestiture decisions should be based to any appreciable extent on exchange-rate trends that may prove to be very short-lived. Some of the recent discussions in the accounting literature on dollar versus foreign currency evaluations include Garda, Lessard and Lorange, and Dietemann.[2] A new Financial Accounting Standards Board (FASB) Exposure Draft also addresses the issue of foreign-currency translation.[3]

Second, of the three objective standards represented by companywide performance, industrywide performance, and economywide performance, the first is the most important. This

TABLE IV.B.1

Performance Evaluation of Managers of Subsidiaries Engaged in International Transfers

Variable	Degree of Importance				Mean	Standard Deviation
	Very (3)	Some (2)	Minor (1)	None (0)		
General Principles						
PEGP1 Financial measures expressed in U.S. dollars	67	21	10	2	2.538	.753
PEGP2 Financial measures expressed in local currency	40	35	17	8	2.077	.947
PEGP3 Standards set by companywide performance	31	38	15	15	1.846	1.036
PEGP4 Standards set by industrywide performance	4	50	25	21	1.365	.864
PEGP5 Standards set by economywide performance	6	44	38	12	1.442	.777
PEGP6 Standards tailored to specific circumstances	27	44	21	8	1.904	.891
PEGP7 Other	0	0	0	100	0	0
Specific Measures						
PESM1 Ratio of profits to equity	33	27	23	17	1.750	1.100
PESM2 Ratio of profits to total assets	52	31	12	6	2.288	.893
PESM3 Ratio of profits to sales	44	40	13	2	2.269	.770
PESM4 Remittances to parent company	12	27	40	21	1.288	.936
PESM5 Net income (profits)	58	29	6	8	2.365	.908
PESM6 Residual income (profits after capital charge)	19	27	25	29	1.365	1.103
PESM7 Sales growth	54	35	8	4	2.385	.796
PESM8 Market share	44	42	8	6	2.250	.837
PESM9 Cost reduction	46	44	10	0	2.365	.658
PESM10 Adherence to budgets	62	29	8	2	2.500	.728
PESM11 Meeting plan goals	63	33	4	0	2.596	.569
PESM12 Production technological innovation	27	44	21	8	1.904	.891
PESM13 New product innovation	25	50	17	8	1.923	.860
PESM14 Other	8	0	0	92	.231	.807

Note: Percent is adjusted to nearest whole number. Sample size is 52 corporations.

may appear a bit chauvinistic in that in a highly diversified company, there may be a great deal more similarity among a given subsidiary operating in a particular industry and other firms operating in that same industry within other conglomerates than there is among the companies within a single conglomerate. Thus, comparing with other firms in the same industry may be more fair than comparing with firms in the same company. The major reason for preferring comparison within the company, however, is probably that a great deal more information is likely to be available on the subsidiaries within the company than there is available on divisions of another company. It is significant also that the subjective standard (standards tailored to specific circumstances) is slightly more important than companywide performance as a basis for performance evaluation. This indicates that at least an attempt is being made to account for the environmental factors that are likely to vary considerably from one subsidiary to the next.

Third, the profit-oriented performance-evaluation measures PESM1 to PESM6 are generally rated as important, but other performance-evaluation criteria are at least as important in an overall sense. The most important criteria are meeting plan goals (PESM11) and adherence to budgets (PESM10). This will please the many authors who insist that the primary instrument of performance evaluation should be a comprehensive system of budgets and goals.[4] Of course, it is apparent that plans usually involve profit goals, so that some of the importance attributed to these criteria may merely reflect the importance of profit. It is also true that such things as sales growth (PESM7) and cost reduction (PESM9) are normally expected to have an ultimately favorable effect on profit. But it is significant that, in an immediate sense, profit is ranked no more highly than other indications of performance, even though it is assumed to be a summary or bottom-line indicator of performance. In the survey of the literature on performance evaluation, it was emphasized that many of the contributors to this literature strongly recommend that corporations diversify their performance evaluation criteria and not lay too much stress on a single profit-based measure such as return on investment (ROI). It would seem that in this respect at least, practice follows prescription.

A matrix of partial correlation coefficients among the performance-evaluation-policy summary variables and the set of exogenous factors is shown in Table IV.B.2. An exhaustive listing of the statistical implications that may be gleaned from this table would be a tedious undertaking, so the discussion will be confined to a partial enumeration of some points that seem more interesting than usual.

TABLE IV.B.2

Partial Correlation Coefficients among Summary Variables Pertaining to Performance-Evaluation Policy and Exogenous Corporate Characteristics and Environmental Variability

	WSAL	SUB	NCOUN	FSUBR	FSALR	CBO1	ENVA
PEGPD	.0443	-.0242	.2123	.0007	-.2228	.2454	.2193
	(.271)	(.438)	(.083)**	(.498)	(.073)**	(.053)**	(.076)**
PEGPO	.2102	-.1572	-.0248	.1582	.0767	.1943	.1948
	(.085)**	(.154)*	(.438)	(.153)*	(.310)	(.103)*	(.103)*
PEGPS	-.1879	.0034	.1451	-.1102	-.1219	.2838	.0590
	(.111)*	(.273)	(.174)*	(.238)	(.215)	(.031)***	(.352)
PESMPR	.1650	.0506	.0565	-.0049	-.1279	.0369	.3541
	(.142)*	(.372)	(.358)	(.487)	(.204)*	(.406)	(.009)***
PESMG	-.2717	-.0254	.1298	.3663	-.3822	.0297	.3399
	(.037)***	(.435)	(.201)*	(.007)***	(.005)***	(.424)	(.012)***
PESMC	-.0565	.0037	.0470	-.0701	0.0656	.1042	.3112
	(.358)	(.490)	(.381)	(.326)	(.336)	(.250)	(.020)***
PESMBG	-.2071	.1057	.1110	-.1801	-.0223	.2787	.5601
	(.089)**	(.247)	(.237)	(.121)*	(.443)	(.033)***	(.001)***
PESMI	.1245	.0921	-.1030	-.0479	-.0021	-.1092	.2609
	(.210)	(.276)	(.253)	(.374)	(.395)	(.240)	(.044)***

Code:

PEGPD	Dollar-oriented performance-evaluation criteria	WSAL	World sales
PEGPO	Objective performance evaluation	SUB	Number of subsidiaries
PEGPS	Subjective performance evaluation	NCOUN	Number of countries in which company operates
PESMPR	Profit-oriented performance evaluation	FSUBR	Ratio of foreign subsidiaries to total subsidiaries
PESMG	Growth-oriented performance evaluation	FSALR	Ratio of foreign sales to total sales
PESMC	Cost-reduction performance evaluation	CBO1	Short-run profit orientation
PESMBG	Budget-goal-oriented performance evaluation	ENVA	Environmental variability
PESMI	Innovation-oriented performance evaluation		

Note: Parentheses indicate significance levels. See page 56 for explication of asterisk use. Sample size is 51 corporations.

One point concerns the apparent tendency of both short-run profit orientation (CBO1) and perceived environmental variability (ENVA) to intensify performance evaluation. All of the statistically significant partial correlation coefficients in the columns pertaining to CBO1 and ENVA are positive. It would seem that all the performance-evaluation criteria are rated more highly the greater the perceived variability of the environment and the greater the orientation to short-run profit. This could conceivably be attributable to personality differentials among the respondents who filled in the questionnaires. The hypothesis would be that low-keyed (placid, philosophical, calm) personalities might tend to give low weightings to nearly everything while high-keyed (excitable, intense, agitated) personalities would have done the opposite. On the other hand, this could reflect an actual, objective phenomenon. Those corporations that are currently doing less comfortably than other corporations might actually apply performance-evaluation standards more harshly and, at the same time, owing to the difficulties currently being encountered, might tend to perceive the external world as less predictable and consequently more threatening.

Turning to the objective variables, there is clearly a tendency for number of countries in which company operates (NCOUN) to intensify performance evaluation while the foreign sales ratio (FSALR) tends to deintensify it. That is, the statistically significant partial correlation coefficients in the NCOUN column are all positive, while the statistically significant coefficients in the FSALR column are all negative. Of course, it was already mentioned that selling overseas is a relatively mild form of foreign involvement relative to having subsidiary companies overseas and operating these subsidiaries in foreign countries. Thus, the number of countries (NCOUN) and foreign sales ratio (FSALR) are two very different structural variables, and it is understandable that in some cases they should work in different directions.

The overall financial scale of the organization (WSAL) turns up as a significant determinant of several of the performance-evaluation variables. Increasing scale tends to increase utilization of objective performance standards and decrease reliance upon subjective standards. This is understandable in that larger scale would tend to reduce the amount of specific information about subsidiary operations that the top management group can be expected to absorb. Large size also tends to diminish emphasis upon sales growth, which is again highly plausible in that there are diminishing returns to everything, including size. The lower emphasis upon budget adherence and goal fulfillment might suggest generally more lenient application of performance-evaluation criteria in large companies. An alternative interpretation, noting the positive and significant effect of world sales (WSAL) on profit-oriented specific measures of performance (PESMPR), would be that greater emphasis upon profit in larger companies is a substitute for reduced reliance upon goals and budgets. This would correspond with the lower reliance in larger companies on subjective standards (PEGPS) owing to the inability of top management in very large firms to take much account of specific circumstances confronting each of the many subsidiary firms (such account being required if the parent company is to participate meaningfully in a detailed specification of budgets and goals).

The result with respect to the effect of world sales (WSAL) on innovation-oriented performance evaluation (PESMI) approaches statistical significance and is worthy of mention. One of the defenses of big business is that large corporations can afford to do more research and, hence, more innovating. The positive effect of size on innovation-oriented performance-evaluation criteria would be consistent with this contention.

Table IV.B.3 is a matrix of simple correlation coefficients among the summary variables relating to performance evaluation. Without exception, the statistically significant correlation coefficients are positive. This suggests that performance evaluation, like subsidiary autonomy, is unidimensional within the corporation. That is, if one performance evaluation criterion is likely to be highly weighted, so also are others. Once again the possibility exists that this situation is purely an artifact based upon some respondents weighting everything more highly than other respondents without there being any objective differences in weighting within their respective corporations. On the other hand, it is certainly not implausible that just as persons may be characterized as high keyed or low keyed, so also may corporations. As was mentioned just above, there is the possibility that corporations that are not doing as well as they would like might tend to become high keyed, that is, for a fairly tense and harsh spirit to develop among the upper executive corps, so that all aspects of performance evaluation become tighter and all components of performance-evaluation criteria become more strictly applied.

To anticipate a bit some results to be shown below, it may be pointed out that one argument against the hypothesis that personality differentials among the respondents tend to make one group weight everything more heavily and another group everything more lightly is that many of the statistically significant correlations among different summary policy variables are in fact negative. If there was indeed a tendency for some respondents to weight

TABLE IV.B.3

Simple Correlation Coefficients among Summary Variables Relating to Performance Evaluation

	PEGPD	PEGPO	PEGPS	PESMPR	PESMG	PESMC	PESMBG	PESMI
PEGPD	1.000							
PEGPO	-.0864 (.275)	1.000						
PEGPS	.1834 (.101)*	-.0039 (.489)	1.000					
PESMPR	.5937 (.001)***	.0086 (.467)	-.0174 (.452)	1.000				
PESMG	.2437 (.044)***	-.0469 (.373)	.2052 (.076)**	.2086 (.073)**	1.000			
PESMC	.2777 (.025)***	-.1059 (.232)	.0813 (.287)	.0913 (.264)	.3618 (.005)***	1.000		
PESMBG	.2941 (.019)***	.2059 (.076)**	.2649 (.032)***	.3152 (.013)***	.3012 (.017)***	.2793 (.025)***	1.000	
PESMI	.3855 (.003)***	.0923 (.262)	.1439 (.159)*	.5139 (.001)***	.1660 (.125)*	.0533 (.357)	.1749 (.112)*	1.000

Code:
PEGPD   Dollar-oriented performance-evaluation criteria
PEGPO   Objective performance-evaluation criteria
PEGPS   Subjective performance-evaluation criteria
PESMPR   Profit-oriented performance-evaluation criteria
PESMG   Growth-oriented performance-evaluation criteria
PESMC   Cost-reduction performance-evaluation criteria
PESMBG   Budget-goal-oriented performance evaluation criteria
PESMI   Innovation-oriented performance-evaluation criteria

Note: Parentheses indicate significance level. See Table III.B1 above for explication. Sample size is 52 corporations.

110

TABLE IV.C.3

Objectives of Instrumental Transfer Pricing
(in percent)

| | Degree of Importance | | | | | Standard |
Specific Objective	High (3)	Medium (2)	Low (1)	None (0)	Mean	Deviation
All companies in sample (52)						
ITPO1	10	15	13	62	.731	1.050
ITPO2	13	6	17	63	.672	1.076
ITPO3	10	21	12	58	.827	1.080
ITPO4	13	15	19	52	.904	1.107
ITPO5	6	12	23	60	.635	.908
ITPO6	10	17	13	60	.769	1.059
ITPO7	4	6	25	65	.481	.779
ITPO8	15	17	4	63	.846	1.195
ITPO9	17	12	10	62	.846	1.195
ITPO10	4	2	0	94	.154	.638

114

everything more heavily, then all or practically all of the correlation coefficients would be positive.

What is particularly interesting about Table IV.B.2 in relation to Table III.C.6, which gave correlations among current business objectives of the overall corporation, is that a trade-off between profit emphasis and emphasis on other goals does not appear. The most striking feature of Table III.C.6 was the negative correlations among short-term profit (CBO1) and all the other goals, with the single exception of sales growth (CBO3). On the basis of the results, with respect to current business objectives, it would have been tempting to hypothesize that in the realm of performance evaluation of subsidiary managers a trade-off would appear between emphasis upon profit (PESMPR) and emphasis upon other goals. For example, one would have expected those corporations that place a great deal of emphasis on profit in performance evaluation to put a correspondingly smaller emphasis on, for example, innovation-oriented criteria (PESMI). But, in fact, the correlation between profit-oriented performance-evaluation criteria (PESMPR) and innovation-oriented performance-evaluation criteria (PESMI) is positive and significant. Apparently, the conflicts in goals at the level of the overall corporation are not reflected in conflicts in performance-evaluation criteria for the subsidiary managers.

C. Findings on Transfer Pricing

Tables IV.C.1, IV.C.2, and IV.C.3 present tabulations of the responses to the transfer-pricing items on the questionnaire. Table IV.C.1 shows that the most important perceived objective of the transfer-pricing system is to increase overall profit. This objective is rated more highly than simplicity and ease of application and facilitate performance evaluation of managers. This result suggests that these latter objectives are perceived more as means to an end rather than an end in themselves. That is, a good system of performance evaluation backed by a consistent transfer-pricing system is a means of earning higher profit.

Table IV.C.2 shows relative usage of the more important transfer-pricing methods. Market price is by far the most important single transfer-pricing method, followed by standard unit full cost plus fixed markup, which is a market-price imitative method. The theoretical transfer-pricing methods TPM9 through TPM12 (marginal cost and so forth) are very little used. Instrumental transfer pricing, which is the term coined in this study to indicate transfer pricing that represents an intervention with the

TABLE IV.C.1

General Objectives of the Transfer-Pricing System
(in percent)

General Objective	Degree of Importance				Mean	Standard Deviation
	Dominant (3)	Very (2)	Somewhat (1)	None (0)		
TPGO1	6	46	35	13	1.442	.802
TPGO2	4	38	33	25	1.212	.871
TPGO3	40	31	13	15	1.962	1.084
TPGO4	4	35	21	40	1.019	.960
TPGO5	10	6	0	85	.404	.975

Code: TPGO1 Simplicity and ease of application
TPGO2 Facilitate performance evaluation of managers
TPGO3 Increase overall corporate profit
TPGO4 Increase overall corporate sales
TPGO5 Other

Note: Percent is adjusted to the nearest whole number. Sample size is 52 corporations.

TABLE IV.C.2

Usage of Various Transfer Pricing Methods
(in percent)

Method	Always Used (4)	Often Used (3)	Sometimes Used (2)	Rarely Used (1)	Never Used (0)	Mean	Standard Deviation
TPM1 Actual unit variable cost	0	2	8	12	79	.327	.706
TPM2 Actual unit full cost	2	6	10	13	69	.579	1.016
TPM3 Standard unit variable cost	0	4	6	17	73	.404	.774
TPM4 Standard unit full cost	6	6	17	12	60	.865	1.237
TPM5 Actual unit variable cost plus fixed markup	0	4	10	12	75	.423	.325
TPM6 Actual unit full cost plus fixed markup	4	13	19	6	58	1.000	1.299
TPM7 Standard unit variable cost plus fixed markup	0	4	10	13	73	.442	.826
TPM8 Standard unit full cost plus fixed markup	12	29	10	10	40	1.615	1.536
TPM9 Marginal cost (incremental cost)	0	0	2	19	79	.231	.469
TPM10 Opportunity cost	0	0	0	13	87	.135	.345
TPM11 Dual pricing	2	2	2	12	83	.288	.776
TPM12 Mathematical programming optimal price	0	0	4	6	90	.135	.444
TPM13 Market price	15	29	23	13	19	2.077	1.355
TPM14 Adjusted market price (less selling costs)	6	25	12	10	48	1.308	1.435
TPM15 Negotiated price (cost plus negotiated markup)	4	13	33	12	38	1.327	1.232
TPM16 Contribution margin	0	2	4	17	77	.308	.643
TPM17 Instrumental price (set by parent company on case-by-case basis to benefit overall corporation)	6	10	13	15	56	.942	1.274
TPM18 No transfer price (free transfers)	0	2	8	4	87	.250	.682
TPM19 Ad hoc transfer price (not based on general policy)	0	6	10	6	79	.423	.893
TPM20 Other	4	2	2	0	92	.250	.905

nearest whole number. Sample size is 52 corporations.

Subset of companies indicating some use
of instrumental pricing (28)

ITPO1	18	29	25	29	1.357	1.096
ITPO2	25	11	32	32	1.286	1.182
ITPO3	18	39	21	21	1.536	1.036
ITPO4	25	29	36	11	1.679	.983
ITPO5	11	21	43	25	1.179	.945
ITPO6	18	32	25	25	1.429	1.069
ITPO7	7	11	46	36	.893	.875
ITPO8	29	32	7	32	1.571	1.230
ITPO9	32	21	18	29	1.571	1.230
ITPO10	7	4	0	89	.286	.854

Code: ITPO1   Take advantage of economies of scale in production
      ITPO2   Provide inexpensive materials for importing subsidiaries
      ITPO3   Stabilize the competitive position of a subsidiary
      ITPO4   Maintain good relations with host countries
      ITPO5   Reduce currency fluctuation losses
      ITPO6   Reduce customs duty payments
      ITPO7   Reduce sales tax payments
      ITPO8   Reduce corporate profits or income taxes
      ITPO9   Avoid restrictions on earnings repatriation
      ITPO10 Other

Note: Percent is adjusted to the nearest whole number.

115

usual transfer-pricing policy in the interest of overall corporate goals (setting of a transfer-price markup or the transfer price itself by the parent company on a case-by-case basis to benefit the overall corporation), is given an intermediate usage rating by the sample of respondents.

The general results with respect to the common transfer-pricing methods are consistent with a large number of other survey studies of transfer-pricing methods such as Piper, Arpan, Greene and Duerr, and Tang.[5] The consistency of the results from this survey with those from others gives us more confidence that the respondents have done a conscientious job of filling out the questionnaire form. This in turn gives us more confidence that the measure obtained for usage of instrumental transfer pricing is indeed a legitimate and accurate measure of relative usage.

Table IV.C.3 is a tabulation of responses to the item category: objectives of instrumental transfer pricing. The first part of the table gives respondents to each multiple choice relative-importance judgment as a percentage of all 52 companies in the sample, while the last part gives the respondents as a percentage of the subset of 28 companies that did indicate some usage of instrumental transfer pricing. A few companies indicated no use of instrumental transfer pricing in the set of items on methods of transfer pricing but then proceeded to rate the objectives of instrumental transfer pricing in the following set of items. These companies were deemed to be making some use of instrumental pricing for purposes of the subset part of the table. Only the absolute values are different between the two parts, not the relative percentages and mean weightings of the specific objectives. With the exception of reduction of sales tax payments (ITPO7), which received a low rating, all of the objectives received about equal weighting. There is no evidence of any single predominant motivation for transfer-price manipulation. These relative-importance ratings may be compared with those found by Tang in his two survey studies.[6] Tang found that Japanese companies placed the highest weights on competitive position of the subsidiaries, currency fluctuations, and restrictions on earnings repatriation, while Canadian companies put the highest ratings on customs duties, competitive position, and restrictions on earnings repatriation.

It should be kept in mind that a large proportion of the companies in the sample said that they did not use instrumental transfer pricing at all, as it was defined on the questionnaire form. Of course, a given company will probably try to adopt a transfer-pricing general policy that is as consistent with as many of these objectives as possible.

The large number of different transfer-pricing methods in use would make an analysis of the determinants of each particular method extremely cumbersome. Therefore, as in the case of the other policy variables, a small set of summary transfer-pricing variables have been defined: TPMMO (market-oriented transfer prices), TPMLO (low transfer prices—based on variable cost and/or eliminating the standard markup), and TPMIN (instrumental transfer pricing). In the case of TPMIN, the variable is defined simply as TPM17 (instrumental transfer pricing), rather than being a combination of like variables as in the other two cases. Table IV.C.4 shows partial correlation coefficients among the three summary policy variables in transfer pricing and the set of exogenous factors. Table IV.C.5 gives the simple correlation coefficients among the set of three summary policy variables.

The fact that all of the simple correlation coefficients are positive might indicate that once again the study is faced with a possible heavy-weighting-of-everything-versus-light-weighting-of-everything problem. However, an examination of the two tables (IV.C.4 and IV.C.5) in conjunction reveals a possibility that indeed something like this is happening with respect to the transfer-pricing judgment, but that it is not a reflection of personality differentials among the respondents that make some of them weight everything heavily and others on them weight everything lightly. Consider the positive correlation in Table IV.C.5 between market-oriented transfer pricing (TPMMO) and instrumental transfer pricing (TPMIN). One would expect there to be an inverse relationship between these two, but the simple correlation coefficient is in fact positive. Turning to Table IV.C.4, however, it can be seen that the variable number of subsidiaries (SUB) is significantly and positively related to both market-oriented transfer prices (TPMMO) and instrumental transfer prices (TPMIN). Upon reflection, this is quite understandable. A company with a large number of subsidiaries will tend to have a large number of transfers between subsidiaries. It may, therefore, use market pricing often and at the same time instrumental pricing often. It is a matter of interpreting "often" in terms of <u>absolute numbers</u> of transfers covered by a certain transfer-pricing method rather than in terms of <u>relative numbers</u>.

It will also be noted from Table IV.C.4 that there are some forces operative that would tend to make market-oriented transfer pricing (TPMMO) and instrumental transfer pricing (TPMIN) inversely correlated, as was expected by this study. In particular, both world sales (WSAL) and environmental variability (ENVA) tend to increase usage of market-oriented transfer prices (TPMMO) while they decrease usage of instrumental transfer prices (TPMIN).

TABLE IV.C.4

Partial Correlation Coefficients among Summary Variables Pertaining to Transfer-Pricing Policy and Exogenous Corporate Characteristics and Environmental Variability

	WSAL	SUB	NCOUN	FSUBR	FSALR	CBO1	ENVA
TPMMO	.2396	.2197	-.2346	.2402	.0433	-.0060	.2564
	(.059)**	(.076)**	(.063)**	(.056)**	(.390)	(.485)	(.046)***
TPMLO	-.1379	.0763	-.1499	.0289	.1938	-.2738	-.0772
	(.186)*	(.311)	(.166)*	(.426)	(.104)*	(.036)***	(.309)
TPMIN	-.2289	.2462	-.1313	.1965	.1099	.1465	-.1387
	(.068)**	(.054)**	(.198)*	(.101)*	(.239)	(.171)*	(.185)*

Code:
TPMMO Market-oriented transfer pricing
TPMLO Low transfer pricing
TPMIN Instrumental transfer pricing
WSAL World sales
SUB Number of subsidiaries
NCOUN Number of countries in which company operates
FSUBR Ratio of foreign subsidiaries to total subsidiaries
FSALR Ratio of foreign sales to total sales
CBO1 Short-run profit orientation
ENVA Environmental variability

Note: Parentheses indicate significance level. See Table III.B.1 above for explication of summary variables. Sample size is 51 corporations.

TABLE IV.C.5

Simple Correlation Coefficients among Summary Variables
Relating to Transfer Pricing

	TPMMO	TPMLO	TPMIN
TPMMO	1.000		
TPMLO	.1562	1.000	
	(.139)*		
TPMIN	.2155	.2313	1.000
	(.066)**	(.053)**	

Code: TPMMO Market-oriented transfer-pricing
TPMLO Low transfer pricing
TPMIN Instrumental transfer pricing
Note: Parentheses indicate significance level. See Table
III.B.1 above for explication of summary variables. Sample size
is 52 corporations.

These two variables (WSAL and ENVA) therefore tend to produce a
negative simple correlation between market-oriented transfer pricing (TPMMO) and instrumental transfer pricing (TPMIN). But they
are overwhelmed by the effects of number of subsidiaries (SUB),
number of countries in which company operates (NCOUN), and ratio
of foreign subsidiaries to total subsidiaries (FSUBR) on market-
oriented transfer pricing (TPMMO) and instrumental transfer
pricing (TPMIN). All of these variables affect market-oriented
transfer pricing (TPMMO) and instrumental transfer pricing
(TPMIN) in the same direction (owing to the fact that they all tend
to produce a large number of transfers as mentioned previously),
and, therefore, they tend to produce a positive simple correlation
among them.

D. Relationships between Autonomy and
Performance Evaluation

Table IV.D.1 is a matrix of simple correlation coefficients
among the summary variables pertaining to autonomy policy and
those pertaining to performance-evaluation policy. It was expected

TABLE IV.D.1

Simple Correlation Coefficients among Summary
Variables Pertaining to Subsidiary Autonomy
and Performance Evaluation Policy

	INSTA	INSTSR	INSTLR	INSTIN
PEGPD	-.1211	-.1257	.0026	-.1681
	(.196)*	(.187)*	(.493)	(.117)*
PEGPO	.0812	.0330	-.0203	.1183
	(.283)	(.408)	(.443)	(.202)*
PEGPS	-.0460	-.1692	-.0124	.0893
	(.373)	(.115)*	(.465)	(.265)
PESMPR	.1726	.1982	.1103	.1211
	(.111)*	(.080)**	(.218)	(.196)*
PESMG	.0324	.0118	-.0083	.1067
	(.410)	(.467)	(.477)	(.226)
PESMC	-.2426	-.2274	-.0007	-.2931
	(.042)***	(.052)**	(.498)	(.017)***
PESMBG	-.0867	-.0814	-.0842	-.0504
	(.270)	(.283)	(.276)	(.361)
PESMI	.1593	.1854	.1795	.0876
	(.130)*	(.094)**	(.101)*	(.269)

Code:

PEGPD	Dollar-oriented performance-evaluation criteria
PEGPO	Objective performance-evaluation criteria
PEGPS	Subjective performance-evaluation criteria
PESMPR	Profit-oriented performance-evaluation criteria
PESMG	Growth-oriented performance-evaluation criteria
PESMC	Cost-reduction performance-evaluation criteria
PESMBG	Budget-goal-oriented performance-evaluation criteria
PESMI	Innovation-oriented performance-evaluation criteria
INSTA	All instruments
INSTSR	Short-run instruments
INSTLR	Long-run instruments
INSTIN	Internal-transaction instruments

Note: Parentheses indicate significance level. See Table
III.B.1 above for explication of summary variables. Sample size
is 52 corporations.

that as more autonomy is granted to the subsidiaries, the tighter
the performance-evaluation standards would have to be in order to
maintain control. Or, looking at the matter from the other direction,
if the parent company is very strict in the application of performance
evaluation, it should grant a great deal of autonomy to the subsidiaries to ensure that each subsidiary is enabled to meet (at least
potentially) the high performance standards.

But, out of 14 correlation coefficients that are statistically
significant, only 7 are positive. It will be noted, however, that of
the seven statistically significant negative correlation coefficients
among performance-evaluation and autonomy variables, three occur
on the row for cost-reduction-oriented performance-evaluation
criteria (PESMC). Upon reflection, it is not surprising that an
emphasis upon cost reduction in the corporation should be inversely
associated with subsidiary autonomy. Cost reduction sometimes
comes about through innovations in production technology that do
not cost jobs but frequently involve the laying off or termination of
employees. This is one of the most difficult things for any company
to do. Therefore, when a subsidiary's costs have to be cut, the
parent company may have to take a more active role in the determination of the cuts, with a consequent reduction in the subsidiary's
independence. It is often commented upon in the management literature that cost reduction frequently must be done in a crisis at-
mosphere in which the usual ideals with respect to decentralization
are often sacrificed. For example, Solomons writes, "As soon as
recession strikes, there is liable to be a reaction. Complete, or
almost complete decentralization is seen to be expensive. Services
are being duplicated."[7]

Although statistically weaker, there is also a negative association between dollar-oriented performance-evaluation criteria
(PEGPD) and three of the four autonomy measures: all instruments
(INSTA), short-run instruments (INSTSR), and long-run instruments
(INSTLR). This might be owing to the effects of short-run profit
orientation (CBO1) on dollar-oriented performance-evaluation criteria (PEGPD) and on the instrument variables (INST). Short-run
profit emphasis (CBO1) decreases autonomy but increases emphasis
upon dollar measures of performance.

E. Relationships between Autonomy and Transfer Pricing

Table IV. E. 1 shows the simple correlation coefficients among
summary variables pertaining to subsidiary sutonomy and transfer
pricing. The expectation that a high degree of autonomy would be
associated with high utilization of market-oriented transfer prices

is confirmed. All four of the simple correlation coefficients between TPMMO (market-oriented transfer-pricing methods) and the four summary variables on subsidiary autonomy (INSTA—all instruments, INSTR—short-run instruments, INSTLR—long-run instruments, and INSTIN—internal-transaction instruments) are positive, and three are statistically significant.

TABLE IV.E.1

Simple Correlation Coefficients among Summary
Variables Pertaining to Subsidiary Autonomy
and Transfer Pricing

	INSTA	INSTSR	INSTLR	INSTIN
TPMMO	.1568	.2289	.2117	.0449
	(.133)*	(.051)**	(.066)**	(.376)
TPMLO	-.0040	.1235	-.1478	.0159
	(.489)	(.191)*	(.148)*	(.456)
TPMIN	-.2063	-.1284	-.1253	-.2178
	(.071)**	(.182)*	(.188)*	(.060)**

Code: TPMMO Market-oriented transfer pricing
   TPMLO Low transfer pricing
   TPMIN Instrumental transfer pricing
   INSTA   All instruments
   INSTSR Short-run instruments
   INSTLR Long-run instruments
   INSTIN Internal-transaction instruments
Note: Parentheses indicate significance level. See Table III.B.1 above for explication of summary variables. Sample size is 52 corporations.

A complementary expectation is that more usage of artificial transfer pricing as reflected by the components of TPMLO (low transfer prices) and in TPMIN (TPM17—instrumental transfer pricing) would necessitate more interference with and less independence for the subsidiaries. There is a verification of this expectation for instrumental transfer pricing (TPMIN). There are negative and statistically significant correlations between instrumental transfer pricing (TPMIN) and all four measures of subsidiary autonomy. The strongest inverse association is between instrumental transfer pricing (TPMIN) and internal-transaction instruments (INSTIN). This is as expected.

On the other hand, there is no confirmation of the expected inverse relationship between artificial transfer prices as contained in TPMLO (low transfer-pricing methods) and subsidiary autonomy. There is a negative correlation between low transfer pricing (TPMLO) and long-run instruments (INSTLR), but this is counterbalanced by a positive correlation between low transfer pricing (TPMLO) and short-run instruments (INSTR). Both correlations are weakly significant. One would expect the strongest inverse association to hold between low transfer pricing (TPMLO) and internal-transaction instruments (INSTIN), but the correlation coefficient between these two variables is negligible.

This result seems sufficiently anomalous to merit inspection of the correlations among the component variables of low transfer-pricing methods (TPMLO) and internal dealing instruments (INSTIN). Internal dealing instruments (INSTIN) are selected because it seems obvious that the greatest restrictions would have to be placed on those instruments pertaining to intracompany dealings if substantial departures from market-imitative transfer pricing are envisioned. The breakdown of correlations between instrumental transfer pricing (TPMIN) and the components of internal dealing instruments (INSTIN) is shown for comparison. Table IV.E.2 contains the simple correlation coefficients among the component variables of low transfer-pricing methods (TPMLO) and internal dealing instruments (INSTIN) and among the component variables of internal dealing instruments (INSTIN) and instrumental transfer pricing TPIN = TPM17).

Looking first to the instrumental-transfer-pricing correlations with components of internal dealing instruments, it can be seen that all components of internal dealing instruments are negatively related to instrumental transfer pricing (TPM1N), but the correlations are stronger for the price variables than for the quantity variables.

Inspection of the simple correlation coefficients among components of low transfer-pricing methods (TPMLO) and components of internal dealing instruments (INSTIN) does not fully clear up the problem. Of the 24 simple correlation coefficients in the matrix, 3 of the 4 statistically significant coefficients are positive. Although there is certainly a conflict between use of non-market-imitative transfer prices and manager autonomy in internal dealings, apparently this conflict is overridden by other relationships so that it does not appear in the observable policy interrelationships. The most likely possibility is that the scale factor is overriding the expected inverse relationship between low transfer prices and

TABLE IV.E.2

Simple Correlation Coefficients between Component Variables of INSTIN, TPMLO, and TPMIN

	TPM1	TPM2	TPM3	TPM4	TPM5	TPM7	TPMIN=TPM17
INST2	-.0480	.0981	-.0556	.2729	.1431	.0023	-.1926
	(.368)	(.244)	(.348)	(.025)***	(.156)*	(.494)	(.086)**
INST3	-.0234	.1461	.0025	-.0059	.0868	.0982	-.2424
	(.435)	(.151)*	(.493)	(.483)	(.270)	(.244)	(.042)***
INST5	-.0114	-.0285	-.1831	-.1028	-.0652	-.0370	-.1225
	(.468)	(.420)	(.097)**	(.234)	(.323)	(.397)	(.193)*
INST6	-.0562	-.0160	-.0420	-.0481	-.0917	.0218	-.1698
	(.346)	(.455)	(.384)	(.367)	(.259)	(.439)	(.114)*

Code: TPM1 Actual unit variable cost
TPM2 Actual unit full cost
TPM3 Standard unit variable cost
TPM4 Standard unit full cost
TPM5 Actual unit variable cost plus fixed markup
TPM7 Standard unit variable cost plus fixed markup
INST2 Price on sales to subsidiaries in same country
INST3 Price on sales to subsidiaries in other countries
INST5 Quantity of items sold to other subsidiaries
INST6 Quantity of items purchased from other subsidiaries
TPM17 Instrumental transfer pricing

Note: Parentheses indicate significance level. See Table III.B.1 above for explication of summary variables.
Sample size is 52 companies.

internal autonomy. In section IV.A. it was found that the scale of the corporation as measured by world sales (WSAL) was positively related to internal autonomy (INSTIN). But this scale variable also increases the number of internal transactions and, hence, the number of times low transfer prices will be used in an absolute sense, thus creating as a statistical artifact a positive relationship between low transfer prices and internal dealing autonomy.

It may be noted that the expected relationship of less autonomy in internal dealings with more use of low transfer prices may be appearing with respect to the INST5 (quantity of items sold to other subsidiaries) and INST6 (quantity of items purchased from other subsidiaries) variables. Note that all but one of the simple correlation coefficients in the rows for INST5 and INST6 do have the expected negative sign. The uniform negativity of the signs may outweigh the consideration that each one of the correlation coefficients (with one exception) is shown to be statistically insignificant.

F. Relationships between Transfer Pricing and Performance Evaluation

A major goal in undertaking this study was to attempt to ascertain empirically the actual accommodations between transfer-pricing policy and performance-evaluation policy in multinational corporations. There has been much discussion in the literature concerning the potential conflicts between using transfer pricing as a tool for increasing the welfare of the overall corporation and maintaining conditions favorable to a fair and equitable performance-evaluation system for subsidiary managers. In particular, artificial transfer prices (that is, transfer prices that depart substantially from the prices that would hold were the two companies involved independent) will tend to affect the measured profitabilities of the subsidiaries involved. An artificially low transfer price will favor the measured profitability of the buying subsidiary and reduce the measured profitability of the selling subsidiary. Some account must be taken of this artifical source of variation in the profitabilities of the two subsidiaries. The managers of the two subsidiaries are likely to disagree on how to account for the influence of the transfer price and, thus, political conflict is generated within the corporation. As this study's interest in the relationships between performance evaluation and transfer pricing is greater than it is in some of the other results presented herein, a larger amount of information and commentary will be presented in this section relative to the other sections of Chapter IV.

Table IV.F.1 is analogous to the previously discussed Tables IV.D.1 and IV.E.1. It gives a matrix of simple correlation coefficients among summary variables pertaining to transfer pricing and summary variables pertaining to performance evaluation. A special interest is in the relationship between profit-oriented performance evaluation (PESMPR) and the usage of transfer-pricing methods. It would seem that a company that weights profit heavily in performance evaluation should at the same time tend to use market-oriented transfer prices (TPMMO), since these interfere the least with the natural distribution of profit among the subsidiaries (the distribution that would tend to occur were the subsidiaries independent firms dealing with one another as separate and sovereign entities). This expectation is in fact verified. The simple correlation coefficient between profit-oriented performance evaluation criteria (PESMPR) and market-oriented transfer pricing (TPMMO) is in fact positive and significant.

By the same token, one would expect those firms that go in more heavily for instrumental pricing to take profit-oriented performance-evaluation criteria relatively less seriously, since the transfer-pricing system tends to alter the distribution of profit among the subsidiaries from the natural basis. This expectation is also confirmed. The simple correlation coefficient between profit-oriented performance evaluation criteria (PESMPR) and instrumental transfer pricing (TPMIN) is negative and highly significant. If one single result had to be picked out of this study as the single most important result, this particular correlation coefficient would probably be it. It seems to indicate that those companies that tend to engage in transfer-pricing policies that affect the distribution of profit among subsidiaries also tend to reduce the emphasis placed upon profit measures in performance evaluation. There is widespread agreement in the literature that this is as it should be. Robbins and Stobaugh, for example, are particularly critical of the fact that often return on investment (ROI) is the primary criterion of performance evaluation, even though transfer-pricing policies often affect the ROIs of the different subsidiaries.[8] Many other authors have issued warnings against failing to account for the effect of corporate transfer-pricing policy on subsidiary outcomes when conducting performance evaluations, among them Fantl and Madison.[9]

From the point of view of the corporation, this accommodation between performance-evaluation policy and transfer-pricing policy will probably seem to be causal ("We have this transfer-pricing policy, therefore we must have this performance-evaluation policy"). But, according to the conceptual framework upon which this study is based, in actual fact, both performance-evaluation

TABLE IV.F.1

Simple Correlation Coefficients among Summary Variables Pertaining to
Performance-Evaluation Policy and Transfer-Pricing Policy

	PEGPD	PEGPO	PEGPS	PESMPR	PESMG	PESMC	PESMBG	PESMI
TPMMO	.0117	.0870	-.1572	.1532	.1152	-.0165	.1732	.3996
	(.468)	(.274)	(.138)*	(.144)*	(.213)	(.455)	(.114)	(.002)***
TPMLO	.0048	.1505	-.1502	.1686	-.0118	-.1111	.0416	-.0275
	(.487)	(.148)*	(.149)*	(.121)*	(.468)	(.221)	(.387)	(.425)
TPMIN	-.1608	.2007	.1231	-.2686	.0850	.0433	.1555	-.2220
	(.132)*	(.081)**	(.197)*	(.030)***	(.279)	(.383)	(.140)*	(.061)**

Code:
TPMMO   Market-oriented transfer pricing
TPMLO   Low transfer pricing
TPMIN   Instrumental transfer pricing
PEGPD   Dollar-oriented performance-evaluation criteria
PEGPO   Objective performance-evaluation criteria
PEGPS   Subjective performance-evaluation criteria
PESMPR Profit-oriented performance-evaluation criteria
PESMG   Growth-oriented performance-evaluation criteria
PESMC   Cost-reduction performance-evaluation criteria
PESMBG Budget-goal-oriented performance-evaluation criteria
PESMI   Innovation-oriented performance-evaluation criteria

Note: Parentheses indicate significance level. See Table III.B.1 above for explication of summary variables.
Sample size is 52 corporations.

policy and transfer-pricing policy are simultaneously determined by the set of exogenous factors. The reason for the positive and negative correlations between profit-oriented performance-evaluation criteria (PESMPR) and respectively market-oriented transfer pricing (TPMMO) and instrumental transfer pricing (TPMIN) can be perceived by looking at the effects of the underlying determinants of all three variables. The following table shows the signs of the statistically significant partial correlation coefficients (at a significance level of 25 percent or better) among market-oriented transfer pricing (TPMMO), profit-oriented performance evaluation criteria (PESMPR), and instrumental transfer pricing (TPMIN) and the set of seven exogenous factors of worldwide sales (WSAL), the number of subsidiaries (SUB), the number of countries (NCOUN), foreign-subsidiary ratio (FSUBR), foreign-sales ratio (FSALR), short-run profit orientation (CBO1), and environmental variability (ENVA). These results are obtained from Tables IV.B.2 and IV.C.4 above.

	WSAL	SUB	NCOUN	FSUBR	FSALR	CBO1	ENVA
TPMMO	+	+	-	+			+
PESMPR	+				-		+
TPMIN	-	+	-	+	+	+	-

The associations that are apparently responsible for the positive simple correlation coefficient between market-oriented transfor pricing (TPMMO) and profit-oriented performance-evaluation criteria (PESMPR) are circled with unbroken ovals, while the associations that are apparently responsible for the negative simple correlation coefficient between instrumental transfer pricing (TPMIN) and profit-oriented performance evaluation criteria (PESMPR) are circled with broken ovals. It will be seen that worldwide sales (WSAL) and environmental variability (ENVA) both have increasing effects on market-oriented transfer pricing (TPMMO) and profit-oriented performance-evaluation criteria (PESMPR), thus tending to make these two variables positively correlated. Worldwide sales (WSAL), foreign sales-ratio (FSALR), and environmental variability (ENVA), on the other hand, have opposed effects on profit-oriented performance-evaluation criteria (PESMPR) and instrumental transfer pricing (TPMIN). These opposed effects of the underlying variables tend to produce the observed negative correlation coefficient between profit-oriented performance-evaluation criteria (PESMPR) and instrumental transfer pricing (TPMIN).

Some of the other results in Table IV.F.1 are worthy of mention. Since there is a negative correlation between profit-oriented performance-evaluation criteria (PESMPR) and instrumental transfer pricing (TPMIN), one might also expect a negative correlation between profit-oriented performance evaluation criteria (PESMPR) and low transfer pricing (TPMLO). The variable TPMLO represents the set of low transfer pricing methods, and it would seem that such prices would affect measured profitability in subsidiaries and hence lead to reduced emphasis upon profit measures in performance evaluation. This expectation, however, is not borne out. The computed simple correlation coefficient between low transfer pricing (TPMLO) and profit-oriented performance-evaluation criteria (PESMPR) is in fact positive and significant.

It could be that a distinction is to be made between low transfer prices as a matter of general policy and low prices for particular instrumental purposes. If the low prices are a matter of general policy and, hence, very frequently applied in intracompany transactions, there is less distortion than when they are only applied on occasion, for specific purposes. In the former case, the attitude might be that everybody must live with the pricing policy, so everyone (on the selling side) faces the same disadvantage. There would therefore be less need to adjust the performance-evaluation criteria in response to the transfer-pricing policy.

Another possibility is that there is a scale factor operative here. The argument already made at the end of the previous section to account for the positive relationship between low transfer pricing (TPMLO) and internal-transaction instruments (INSTIN) would follow. Table IV.B.2 shows that world sales (WSAL), the basic measure of financial scale, tends to increase reliance upon the profit-based measures of performance. But scale will also increase the <u>absolute</u> number of times that low transfer prices are used, and this factor might overwhelm the tendency for profit measures to be used less intensively as low transfer prices are used relatively more within a corporation of given size, insofar as observable relationships are concerned. It is also worth mentioning in this context that the actual usage of the transfer pricing methods included in low transfer pricing (TPMLO) is relatively light when compared with other methods, including instrumental pricing. Thus, the expected statistical relationships do not have as much chance of coming to the surface.

It might be hypothesized that those companies that tend to use instrumental pricing more would have for some reason less intense performance evaluation in <u>all</u> categories, including the profit category, and that <u>relatively</u> speaking these companies put just as much emphasis on profit as companies that do not use instrumental pricing so much. But, it will be noticed in Table IV.F.1 that of the six correlation coefficients on the line pertaining to instrumental transfer pricing (TPMIN) that are shown as statistically significant, three are positive. This suggests that some criteria are regarded as more important by firms engaging in instrumental transfer pricing than by other firms, so that it is <u>not</u> a matter of generally less stringent performance-evaluation standards in the former firms.

The results concerning the relationship between transfer-pricing policies and profit-oriented performance-evaluation criteria are sufficiently important that additional information is provided on the relationships between the <u>components</u> of the summary policy variables profit-oriented performance-evaluation criteria (PESMPR), market-oriented transfer pricing (TPMMO), low transfer pricing (TPMLO), and instrumental transfer pricing (TPMIN). This will provide some insight into which particular factors are responsible for the relationships among the summary variables. Table IV.F.2 is a matrix of simple correlation coefficients among the components of the four summary variables involved. Inspection of this table should clarify why the device of the summary variable was adopted. Essentially, the three correlations between PESMPR and TPMMO, PESMPR and TPMLO, and PESMPR and TPMIN in Table IV.F.1 are an attempt to summarize the information contained in the 72 correlation coefficients in Table IV.F.2.

With respect to instrumental transfer pricing (TPMIN = TPM17), it is seen that the overall negative correlation comes from the negative correlation between this variable and the ratio measures of profitability. The positive correlation between market-oriented transfer pricing (TPMMO) and profit-oriented performance-evaluation criteria (PESMPR) comes principally from the positive correlation between ratio of profits to assets (PESM2) and actual unit full cost plus fixed markup (TPM6). It is interesting to note that there are in fact some statistically significant negative correlations among component variables of profit-oriented performance-evaluation (PESMPR) and market-oriented transfer-pricing methods (TPMMO), as, for example, between market price (TPM13) and net income (PESM5); but these are outweighed by the very tight positive correlation between ratio of profits to assets (PESM2) and actual unit full cost plus fixed markup (TPM6), plus some other positive correlations.

Table IV.F.3 is given in order to suggest the abundance of results (perhaps overabundance of results) that would have piled up had the summary-variable approach not been utilized. Table IV.F.3 is an exhaustive listing of every statistically significant simple correlation coefficient between a transfer-pricing method and a performance-evaluation criterion. Included on this list are the high positive correlation between actual unit full cost plus fixed markup (TPM6) and ratio of profits to assets (PESM2) that gave the positive correlation between profit-oriented performance-evaluation criteria

TABLE IV.F.2

Simple Correlation Coefficients among Profit-Oriented Performance-Evaluation
Criteria and Transfer-Pricing Methods That are Components of
Transfer-Pricing Summary Variables

	PESM1	PESM2	PESM3	PESM4	PESM5	PESM6
TPMMO						
TPM6	-.0137	.4058	-.0196	.0645	.1330	-.0274
	(.462)	(.001)***	(.445)	(.325)	(.174)*	(.424)
TPM8	-.0232	-.0605	-.0599	.0105	.1308	.0961
	(.435)	(.335)	(.336)	(.471)	(.178)*	(.249)
TPM13	-.1446	-.0673	-.0766	-.0178	.1826	.0202
	(.153)*	(.318)	(.295)	(.450)	(.098)**	(.444)
TPM14	-.0124	.1130	-.0587	.0786	.0324	.1505
	(.465)	(.312)	(.340)	(.290)	(.410)	(.143)*
TPM15	.1048	.1977	-.1153	.0356	.2066	.1412
	(.230)	(.080)**	(.208)*	(.401)	(.071)**	(.159)*
TPMLO						
TPM1	-.0189	-.0592	-.0208	-.0565	-.0547	.1205
	(.447)	(.338)	(.442)	(.345)	(.350)	(.197)*
TPM2	.0614	.2667	-.0270	-.0753	-.1495	.0182
	(.333)	(.028)***	(.425)	(.298)	(.145)*	(.449)
TPM3	.0288	-.0300	.0772	.1068	.1208	.1913
	(.420)	(.416)	(.293)	(.226)	(.197)*	(.087)**
TPM4	.3637	.1423	.0182	-.0335	.2017	.0655
	(.004)***	(.157)*	(.449)	(.407)	(.076)**	(.322)
TPM5	.0540	-.0358	.0024	-.1104	.1037	.1931
	(.352)	(.400)	(.493)	(.218)	(.232)	(.085)**
TPM7	.0809	.0097	-.1292	.0346	.0940	.1634
	(.284)	(.473)	(.181)*	(.404)	(.254)	(.124)*
TPMIN						
TPM17	-.4020	-.3989	-.3036	-.0844	-.0661	.1129
	(.002)***	(.002)***	(.014)***	(.276)	(.321)	(.213)

Code:

TPMMO	Market-oriented transfer pricing
TPM6	Actual unit full cost plus markup
TPM8	Standard unit full cost plus markup
TPM13	Market price
TPM14	Adjusted market price
TPM15	Negotiated price
TPMLO	Low transfer pricing
TPM1	Actual unit variable cost
TPM2	Actual unit full cost
TPM3	Standard unit variable cost
TPM4	Standard unit full cost
TPM5	Actual unit variable cost plus markup
TPM7	Standard unit variable cost plus markup
TPMIN=TPM17	Instrumental transfer price
PESM1	Ratio of profits to equity
PESM2	Ratio of profits to assets
PESM3	Ratio of profits to sales
PESM4	Remittances to parent company
PESM5	Net income
PESM6	Residual income (profits after capital charge)

Note: Parentheses indicate significance level. Sample size is 52 corporations.

TABLE IV.F.3

List of All Statistically Significant Simple Correlation
Coefficients among Transfer-Pricing Methods and
Performance-Evaluation Criteria

Acronym	Variable	Simple Correlation Coefficient	Significance Level
TPM1	Actual unit variable cost		
PEGP3	Standards set by company-wide performance	.1772	.104
TPM2	Actual unit full cost		
PEGP3	Standards set by companywide performance	.1976	.080
PESM2	Ratio of profits to total assets	.2667	.028
PESM11	Meeting plan goals	.1734	.109
PESM12	Production technological innovation	-.1973	.080
TPM3	Standard unit variable cost		
PEGP2	Financial measures expressed in local currency	-.2307	.050
PEGP6	Standards tailored to specific circumstances	-.1985	.079
PESM6	Residual income	.1913	.087
TPM4	Standard unit full cost		
PEGP3	Standards set by companywide performance	.2741	.025
PESM1	Ratio of profits to equity	.3637	.004
PESM5	Net income	.2017	.076
TPM5	Actual unit variable cost plus fixed markup		
PEGP2	Financial measures expressed in local currency	.2087	.069
PESM6	Residual income	.1931	.085
PESM8	Market share	.1846	.095
PESM12	Production technological innovation	-.1836	.096
PESM13	New product innovation	-.2021	.075
TPM6	Actual unit full cost plus fixed markup		
PEGP2	Financial measures expressed in local currency	.2871	.020
PEGP3	Standards set by companywide performance	.1894	.089
PEGP6	Standards tailored to specific circumstances	-.2033	.074
PESM2	Ratio of profits to total assets	.4058	.001
PESM11	Meeting plan goals	.2122	.065
PESM13	New product innovation	.1756	.106

132

Acronym	Variable	Simple Correlation Coefficient	Significance Level
TPM7	Standard unit variable cost plus fixed markup		
PEGP4	Standards set by industrywide performance	.2361	.046
PESM7	Sales growth	-.2041	.073
PESM13	New product innovation	.1863	.092
TPM8	Standard unit full cost plus fixed markup		
PEGP3	Standards set by companywide performance	.2701	.026
PESM8	Market share	.2287	.051
PESM10	Adherence to budgets	.1930	.085
PESM11	Meeting plan goals	.3572	.005
TPM9	Marginal cost		
PEGP1	Financial measures expressed in U.S. dollars	-.1921	.086
PESM3	Ratio of profits to sales	-.1753	.107
PESM7	Sales growth	-.2423	.042
TPM10	Opportunity cost		
PEGP6	Standards tailored to specific circumstances	-.2124	.065
PESM7	Sales growth	-.1925	.086
PESM9	Cost reduction	-.2213	.057
TPM11	Dual pricing		
PEGP2	Financial measures expressed in local currency	-.2178	.060
PEGP3	Standards set by companywide performance	.2271	.053
PEGP6	Standards tailored to specific circumstances	-.2427	.041
PESM6	Residual income	.2182	.060
PESM12	Production technological innovation	.2111	.067
PESM13	New product innovation	.2308	.043
TPM12	Mathematical programming optimal price		
PEGP2	Financial measures expressed in local currency	-.2117	.066
PESM9	Cost reduction	-.3731	.003
PESM11	Meeting plan goals	-.2462	.039
TPM13	Market price		
PEGP2	Financial measures expressed in local currency	-.4021	.002

(continued)

Table IV.F.3, continued

Acronym	Variable	Simple Correlation Coefficient	Significance Level
PEGP3	Standards set by companywide performance	-.2148	.063
PESM5	Net income	-.1826	.098
PESM7	Sales growth	-.4278	.001
PESM8	Market share	-.4320	.001
PESM11	Meeting plan goals	-.2385	.044
TPM14	Adjusted market price (market price less selling costs)		
PEGP2	Financial measures expressed in local currency	.1843	.095
PESM12	Production technological innovation	.3607	.004
PESM13	New product innovation	.3056	.014
TPM15	Negotiated price (cost plus negotiated markup)		
PEGP2	Financial measures expressed in local currency	.2134	.064
PESM2	Ratio of profits to total assets	.1977	.080
PESM5	Net income	.2066	.071
PESM8	Market share	.2803	.022
PESM9	Cost reduction	-.1745	.108
PESM13	New product innovation	.4129	.001
TPM16	Contribution margin		
PESM1	Ratio of profits to equity	.2495	.037
PESM6	Residual income	.2531	.035
PESM8	Market share	.1821	.098
PESM12	Production technological innovation	.1895	.089
TPM17	Instrumental transfer pricing		
PEGP1	Financial measures expressed in U.S. dollars	-.1917	.087
PESM1	Ratio of profits to equity	-.4020	.002
PESM2	Ratio of profits to total assets	-.3986	.002
PESM3	Ratio of profits to sales	-.3036	.014
PESM11	Meeting plan goals	.2106	.067
PESM12	Production technological innovation	-.1949	.083
PESM13	New product innovation	-.2010	.077
TPM18	No transfer price (free transfers)		
TPM19	Ad hoc transfer price (not based on general policy)		
PESM6	Residual income	.1783	.103

Note: Sample size is 52 corporations.

(PESMPR) and market-oriented transfer pricing (TPMMO) and the high negative correlations between instrumental transfer pricing (TPMIN = TPM17) and respectively ratio of profits to equity (PESM1), ratio of profits to assets (PESM2), and ratio of profits to sales (PESM3) that gave the negative correlation between instrumental transfer pricing (TPMIN) and profit-oriented performance-evaluation criteria (PESMPR). It is seen that these particular coefficients are practically buried in a mass of information. One might browse through a table such as Table IV. F. 3 picking out a few pieces here and there of possibly interesting information, but on the whole it is not a tool well suited to meaningful analysis of the problems studied in this research.

Another tool unsuited to a project such as this in which there are a great many potential relationships is the cross-tabulation table. Table IV. F. 4 shows first a cross-tabulation of instrumental transfer pricing (TPMIN = TPM17) with ratio of profits to assets (PESM2) and last a cross-tabulation of actual unit full cost plus fixed markup (TPM6) with ratio of profits to total assets (PESM2). Relationships between two variables in a cross-tabulation all perceived by looking for a pattern or "cluster" of the observations, either along the downward-sloping diagonals (for a positive relationship) or along the upward-sloping diagonals (for a negative relationship). Unless the relationship is very obvious, however, it will be extremely difficult to pick it out of a cross-tabulation table. The two cases shown have simple correlation coefficients that are highly significant statistically, yet there is no pattern immediately visible to the eye.

There is also a basic economy consideration. The simple correlation coefficient sums up the information in a crosstabs table in a single number. In view of the fact that we have considered in the foregoing many dozens of simple correlation coefficients, it is apparent that presenting a cross-tabulation table for every one of these coefficients would have produced an overwhelming and completely indigestible mass of numbers.

TABLE IV.F.4

Cross-Tabulations of PESM2 with TPM17 and TPM6
(in percent)

Ratio of profits to total assets (PESM2)	Always Used (4)	Often Used (3)	Sometimes Used (2)	Rarely Used (1)	Never Used (0)
Instrumental pricing (TPM17)					
Very Important (3)	1.9	0.0	5.8	9.6	34.6
Some Importance (2)	1.9	5.8	3.8	1.9	17.3
Minor Importance (1)	0.0	3.8	0.0	3.8	3.8
No Importance (0)	1.9	0.0	3.8	0.0	0.0
Simple correlation coefficient = $-.398$					
Significance level = .002					
Actual unit full cost plus fixed markup (TPM6)					
Very Important (3)	2.8	9.6	15.4	1.9	21.2
Some Importance (2)	0.0	3.8	3.8	1.9	21.2
Minor Importance (1)	0.0	0.0	0.0	1.9	9.6
No Importance (0)	0.0	0.0	0.0	0.0	5.8
Simple correlation coefficient = .435					
Significance level = .001					

Note: Percent is rounded to the nearest whole number. Sample size is 52 corporations.

136

NOTES

1. Elwood L. Miller, Accounting Problems of Multinational Companies (Lexington, Ma.: D. C. Heath, 1979), p. 174.

2. J. A. Garda, "The Measurement of Financial Data in Evaluating Overseas Managerial Efficiency," International Journal of Accounting 12 (Fall, 1976):13-17; Donald R. Lessard and Peter Lorange, "Currency Changes and Management Control: Resolving the Centralization/Decentralization Dilemma," Accounting Review 52 (July 1977):628-37; and Gerald R. Dietemann, "Evaluating Multinational Performance under FASB No. 8," Management Accounting 61 (May 1980):49-55.

3. Financial Accounting Standards Board, Exposure Draft, Foreign-Currency Translation (New York: FASB, August 28, 1980).

4. Sidney M. Robbins and Robert B. Stobaugh, "The Bent Measuring Stick for Foreign Subsidiaries," Harvard Business Review 51 (September-October 1973):80-88, and Bruce D. Henderson and John Dearden, "New System for Divisional Control," ibid. 44 (September-October 1966):144-60.

5. A. G. Piper, "Internal Trading," Accountancy 80 (October 1969):733-36; Jeffrey S. Arpan, International Intracorporate Pricing: Non-American Systems and Views (New York: Praeger, 1972); James H. Greene and Michael G. Duerr, Intercompany Transactions in the Multinational Firm (New York: The Conference Board, 1970); and Roger Y. W. Tang, Transfer-Pricing Practices in the U.S. and Japan (New York: Praeger, 1979).

6. Roger Y. W. Tang, Transfer-Pricing Practices and "Canadian Transfer-Pricing Practices," CA Magazine 13 (March 1980):32-38.

7. David Solomons, Divisional Performance: Measurement and Control (Homewood, Il.: Richard D. Irwin, 1965), p. 15.

8. Robbins and Stobaugh, "Bent Measuring Stick," p. 82.

9. Irving L. Fantl, "Transfer Pricing—Tread Carefully," CPA Journal 44 (December 1974):45, and Roland L. Madison, "Responsibility Accounting and Transfer Pricing: Approach with Caution," Management Accounting 60 (January 1979):29.

5

SUMMARY
AND
CONCLUSIONS

The focus of this study has been on determinants of and inter-relationships among three dimensions of policy in multinational corporations. The three dimensions of interest have been policy with respect to subsidiary autonomy (decentralization), policy with respect to performance evaluation of subsidiary managers, and policy with respect to transfer pricing.

According to the conceptual framework on which the study has been based, all three dimensions of corporate policy are determined by a set of exogenous factors, including corporate characteristics in scale and structure that are fixed in the short run, and environmental conditions. These underlying causal influences create a pattern of association (or accommodation) among the policy dimensions that has the appearance of being of a causal nature to the participants in the process.

An attempt has been made to assess both the associational and causal patterns by means of data collected from a survey of headquarters units of U.S. multinational corporations. The 52 corporations completing the survey questionnaire represent 14.5 percent of the corporations contacted. The sample contains a wide range of variation both with respect to scale of operation and extent of involvement in foreign operations.

Information was collected in four general areas: (1) policy with respect to subsidiary autonomy, (2) policy with respect to performance evaluation, (3) policy with respect to transfer pricing, and (4) exogenous factors relating to corporate characteristics and the external environment. A large number of items were queried in each area.

This research has provided descriptive information on the nature of the responses in each area (see Table I.B.3). There are few surprises in this information, as many of these matters have been covered in prior surveys, and in general the results of this survey are consistent with the prior surveys.

The value of collecting information in the four areas is that it permits exploration of the empirical relationships between and among the four areas. The novelty of this study is that it investigates these interrelationships far more thoroughly than any prior survey study.

From the conceptual framework, it is expected that exogenous factors relating to corporate characteristics and the external environment will have a causal impact on policy with respect to subsidiary autonomy, performance evaluation, and transfer pricing. The relationships among these latter items are viewed as associational rather than causal.

Because of the large number of items queried, an exhaustive report of the possible relationships to be derived from the survey responses would be so voluminous as to overwhelm the absorptive capacity of any reader of it. This consideration motivated the device of the summary variable. Responses were weighted numerically, and closely allied policy variables were combined (by the process of arithmetic averaging) into a much smaller set of summary variables. Similarly the set of exogenous factors was boiled down to a set of seven key factors, including world sales (WSAL), number of subsidiaries (SUB), number of countries in which the multinational operates (NCOUN), foreign subsidiary ratio (FSUBR), foreign sales ratio (FSALR), short-run profit orientation (CBO1), and environmental variability (ENVA). The relatively small set of policy summary variables and the relatively small set of key exogenous factors have been used throughout Chapter 4 to report results.

Causal relationships among the seven key exogenous factors and the policy summary variables have been assessed using the statistical tool of partial correlation. Associational relationships among the policy summary variables have been assessed using the statistical tool of simple correlation.

Tables V.1 and V.2 are an attempt to convey a broad impression of the results in a very condensed format. These are tables of signs of correlation coefficients that have been found to be statistically significant at the level of 25 percent or better. A + indicates that the particular relationship is positive (higher X is associated with higher Y) and a – indicates that the particular relationship is negative (higher X is associated with lower Y). Since this study deals with a very basic form of statistical analysis, a conclusion about the direction of a relationship is about all that can be reasonably hoped for. Therefore, the numerical information has been suppressed in the interest of clarifying the indicated directions of the relationships. If a cell in the table is vacant (does not have either a + or a - in it), then the statistical indications are not clear enough for a judgment to be made, even on the direction of the relationship. Statistically speaking, therefore, there is no evidence of any relationship, either positive or negative.

Tables V.1 and V.2 have been compiled from the appropriate tables in Chapter 4. The following schema indicates the location of each table that has been incorporated into Tables V.1 and V.2:

Partial correlations, causal relationships
(Table V.1)

	Exogenous factors
Autonomy	IV.A.3
Performance Evaluation	IV.B.2
Transfer Pricing	IV.C.4

Simple correlations, associational relationships
(Table V.2)

	Autonomy	Performance Evaluation	Transfer Pricing
Autonomy	IV.A.2	X	X
Performance Evaluation	IV.D.1	IV.B.3	X
Transfer Pricing	IV.E.1	IV.F.1	IV.C.5

The inferences to be drawn from Tables V.1 and V.2 will now be concisely summarized. First of all, a good number of statistically significant results have been ascertained (bearing in mind, of course, that a very generous definition of "statistical significance" has been used throughout this study). The relative success in this respect promotes a greater level of confidence in both the conceptual framework of the study and the reliability and accuracy of the responses received to the questionnaire survey.

Determinants of Autonomy Policy

Size as measured by world sales (WSAL) and perceived environmental variability as measured by ENVA have a positive effect on subsidiary autonomy in overall terms. However, autonomy with respect to internal transfers between subsidiaries is inversely affected by two measures of foreign involvement: number of countries in which the multinational operates (NCOUN) and foreign-subsidiary ratio (FSUBR). This is consistent with multinational firms making

TABLE V.1

Summary of Statistically Significant Relationships among
Summary Policy Variables and Exogenous Factors
(statistically significant at .250 or above)

Policy Variable	WSAL	SUB	NCOUN	FSUBR	FSALR	CBO1	ENVA
INSTA	+		−			−	+
INSTSR					+		+
INSTLR	+					−	
INSTIN	+	+	−	−	+	−	+
PEGPD			+		−	+	+
PEGPO	+	−		+		+	+
PEGPS	−		+	−	−	+	
PESMPR	+				−		+
PESMG	−		+	+	−		+
PESMC						+	+
PESMBG	−		+	−		+	+
PESMI	+					−	+
TPMMO	+	+	−	+			+
TPMLO	−		−		+	−	
TPMIN	−	+	−	+	+	+	−

Code:

INSTA	All instrument variables
INSTSR	Short-run instruments
INSTLR	Long-run instruments
INSTIN	Internal instruments
PEGPD	Dollar-oriented performance evaluation criteria
PEGPO	Objective performance-evaluation criteria
PEGPS	Subjective performance-evaluation criteria
PESMPR	Profit-oriented performance-evaluation criteria
PESMG	Growth-oriented performance evaluation
PESMC	Cost-oriented performance evaluation
PESMBG	Budget-goal-oriented performance evaluation
PESMI	Innovation-oriented performance evaluation
TPMMO	Market-oriented transfer pricing methods
TPMLO	Low transfer-pricing methods
TPMIN	Instrumental transfer pricing
WSAL	World sales
SUB	Number of subsidiaries
NCOUN	Number of countries
FSUBR	Foreign subsidiary ratio
FSALR	Foreign sales ratio
CBO1	Short-run profit orientation
ENVA	Environmental variability

Note: Sample size is 52 corporations.

TABLE V.2

Summary of Statistically Significant Relationships
among Summary Policy Variables
(statistically significant at .250 level)

	INSTA	INSTSR	INSTLR	INSTIN	PEGPD	PEGPO	PEGPS	PESMPR	PESMG	PESMC	PESMBG	PESMI	TPMMO	TPMLO	TPMIN
INSTA															
INSTSR	+														
INSTLR	+	+													
INSTIN	+	+	+												
PEGPD	−	−		−											
PEGPO				+											
PEGPS		−			+										
PESMPR	+	+	+	+	+										
PESMG					+		+	+							
PESMC	−	−		−	+	−			+						
PESMBG					+	+	+	+	+	+					
PESMI	+	+	+		+		+	+	+		+				
TPMMO	+	+	+				−	+	+		+	+			
TPMLO		+	−			+	−	+			−		+		
TPMIN	−	−	−	−	−	+	+	−			+	−	+	+	

Code:
INSTA	All instrument variables
INSTSR	Short-run instruments
INSTLR	Long-run instruments
INSTIN	Internal instruments
PEGPD	Dollar-oriented performance evaluation criteria
PEGPO	Objective performance-evaluation criteria
PEGPS	Subjective performance-evaluation criteria
PESMPR	Profit-oriented performance-evaluation criteria
PESMG	Growth-oriented performance evaluation
PESMC	Cost-oriented performance evaluation
PESMBG	Budget-goal-oriented performance evaluation
PESMI	Innovation-oriented performance evaluation
TPMMO	Market-oriented transfer pricing methods
TPMLO	Low transfer pricing
TPMIN	Instrumental transfer pricing

Note: Sample size is 52 corporations.

more use of transfer pricing for instrumental purposes than domestic firms of similar size, such usage requiring constraints on the flexibility of subsidiaries with respect to transfers.

Determinants of Performance Evaluation Policy

Perceived environmental variability (ENVA) and a short-run profit orientation (CBO1) tend to tighten up performance evaluation, except that short-run profit orientation reduces emphasis upon innovation-oriented criteria. The effect of the other exogenous determinants of performance-evaluation policy is more mixed and complicated. For example, financial size as measured by world sales (WSAL) increases use of objective criteria and decreases use of subjective criteria, increases emphasis upon profit measures and reduces emphasis upon growth and budget-and-goal evaluation, and finally increases emphasis upon innovation. The most obvious interpretation is that larger firms are less able to account for specific circumstances confronting specific subsidiaries, and, hence, go in more for a simpler system of profit-oriented performance evaluation than for the more complicated budget-and-goal approach.

Determinants of Transfer-Pricing Policy

In general, it would be expected that size factors would favor the use of market pricing (considering the above-mentioned influence of size on performance evaluation), while extent of foreign involvement would favor departures from market pricing (because of the larger number of opportunities for profit-enhancing transfer-price manipulation in the international context). There is some verification of this expectation, but a scale factor seems to be complicating the statistical picture. A large firm with many subsidiaries will have many intracompany transfers so that it might legitimately report frequent usage of market pricing and frequent usage of instrumental pricing.

Interrelationships among Autonomy Variables

These are uniformly positive, indicating that if a given firm grants greater autonomy to its subsidiaries in one area, it will also grant greater autonomy in other areas.

Interrelationships among Performance-Evaluation Variables

These are practically all positive, indicating that if a firm rates one criterion highly in performance evaluation, it is likely to rate other criteria highly also. Firms seem therefore more capable of differentiation on the basis of whether their performance evaluation is stringent or lenient than on the basis of differing structures of their performance-evaluation systems. There is no indication of the trade-offs in performance evaluation that one would expect from the existence of trade-offs among current business objectives (compare Tables III.C.6 and IV.B.3).

Interrelationships among Transfer-Pricing Variables

These are all positive. Since there is clearly a trade-off in terms of relative usage of market-oriented prices and non-market-oriented prices, the failure of the statistical computations to reveal this effect must be owing to the scale factor mentioned above.

Relationships between Autonomy and Performance Evaluation

One would expect that more autonomy would require stronger performance evaluation. Although the statistical results are fairly weak in this area, there are some indications that this expectation is correct—except in the cost-reduction criterion. Strong emphasis on cost reduction conflicts with subsidiary autonomy, most probably because cost reduction is frequently difficult since it often entails the elimination of jobs.

Relationships between Autonomy and Transfer Pricing

As expected, market-oriented transfer pricing is positively related to subsidiary autonomy. An expected inverse association between instrumental pricing and subsidiary autonomy was also confirmed. The failure to find a statistically significant inverse relationship between low transfer prices and internal-dealing autonomy is probably owing to a scale factor.

Relationships between Transfer Pricing and Performance Evaluation

The most important result in this area is that profit-oriented performance evaluation is positively associated with market-oriented transfer pricing but inversely associated with instrumental transfer pricing. This suggests that corporations do indeed adjust their performance-evaluation policy to accommodate their transfer-pricing objectives. If transfer pricing is being used as an active tool for overall corporate profit enhancement, even though this causes an artificial distribution of profit among subsidiaries, the corporation will tend to modify its performance-evaluation methods to decrease emphasis upon the profit criterion. This result was described as probably the most important single result forthcoming from the study. It should serve to allay the fears of several authors that corporations blithely ignore the distorting effects of their transfer-pricing policies on the profits of the various subsidiaries when carrying out performance evaluations.

It must be said in conclusion that this study suffers far more than most from the usual defects of statistical analysis. An uncommonly generous standard of statistical significance has been used throughout. By the ordinary 5 percent and 1 percent standards, very few of the results shown would have merited the judgment of statistical significance. Moreover, the test of significance that has been used depends on the assumption of normality in the underlying data, and it is very doubtful that this assumption is completely accurate. The implication is that the probability of Type I error is an underestimate of the true probability. Also, it will be noted that the arithmetic size of the correlation coefficients is small, even when they are shown as statistically significant. For example, a correlation coefficient of .250 has a corresponding R^2 of only .0625. That is, only 6.25 percent of the variation in Y can be statistically explained by the variation in X. Obviously many other factors are involved that this study has not taken into account.

All of this adds up to an emphatic caveat concerning the validity of the results obtained. There is no denying that at best things are perceived "through a glass darkly."

On the other hand, there is much to recommend the notion that imperfect knowledge is better than no knowledge. Up to this point, discussion of the interrelationships among the various policy areas of interest to this study has been completely hypothetical and conjectural. The empirical content has been confined to a few real-world cases that may or may not be illustrative of general conditions. Although highly imperfect in its nature, it seems apparent that the empirical evidence accumulated by the survey and reported here represents an improvement over past discussion, at least as far as empirics are concerned.

It is hoped by the author that the results reported in this study will be of interest not only to academic accountants and management analysts but also to the middle- and upper-level executives whose task it is to administer the large multinational enterprises that handle such a large proportion of the total economic activity in our contemporary world society. In a world in which two-thirds of the population subsists in conditions of abysmal poverty (relative to the standards set in a few rich nations such as the United States), it is vitally important that the maximum productive output be extracted from the economic resources available to the human population. The executive corps will be making its contribution toward this objective by adopting a highly professional attitude toward their work.

It is somewhat ironic that although the administration of organizations is as old as human civilization, the art and science of administration is one of the least developed of the professions. Most of those fields recognized as professional, such as law, medicine, science, engineering, accounting, and so on, possess large bodies of empirical information and theoretical formulations that are constantly being expanded by voluminous professional literatures. To some extent, of course, effective administration draws on the tools and findings of the more traditional and well-organized professions. But, at the same time, there is currently being developed a theoretical and empirical literature, exemplified by the present study, devoted specifically to the professional problems of administration. It is essential that the real-world executive corps avail itself of this growing literature in order to attain a higher level of professional skill.

To take maximum advantage of the professional literature in administration, it will probably be necessary for managers to become more familiar with statistical and mathematical methodologies and tools. Much of the "pop" business literature manages to evade even numbers, to say nothing of mathematics and statistics, but the price is that it often conveys little beyond vague generalities and fuzzy prescriptions whose practical value is liable to be severely limited. In order to deal effectively with modern business problems, it is not enough simply to have a broad appreciation of the multitude of factors bearing on these problems. It is also necessary to have strong analytical powers based upon a developed capacity for formal abstraction, so that the bearings of the various factors on the problems may be accurately assessed. Good instincts are very helpful, of course, but more often than not good instincts are based on a careful analysis that strips a given problem down to a manageable decision issue.

Studies such as this one are providing a theoretical and empirical foundation that will ultimately enable administration to be conducted in a more effective manner. This statement is certainly not to be construed as an assault on the present level of competence in corporate administration. To say that things could be better is not to say that they are bad now. In fact, it has been frequently commented here that by and large, corporate policy formulation empirically does seem to follow the prescriptions set forth in the professional management literature. The most striking example of this is in the smaller weighting given to profit measures in performance evaluation when the multinational firm makes heavy use of instrumental transfer-pricing methods, which, in effect, artificially redistribute profits among the subsidiaries. The fact that these results are often statistically weak as well as numerically

small can easily be attributed to problems of measurement and complex interactions that can only be very imperfectly countered with
the survey methods and statistical analysis currently available.

On the other hand, at least a part of the statistical weakness
and numerical smallness can with little doubt be attributed to imperfections in the management process within multinational corporations—such imperfections caused, at least in part, by an inadequate
level of professionalism in the executive corps. Certainly most
managers will admit that there exists a random, arbitrary, and
capricious element in real-world administration, and while opinions
may differ as to what part of this random element is potentially con-
trollable and what part is fundamentally inevitable, most will agree
that there is room for improvement. The investigator has done her
part in making the survey, analyzing it, and presenting the results.
It is now up to readers working in corporate administration to study
these results, in order that they may make a contribution to the
formulation of sound corporate policy in the areas of transfer pricing
and performance evaluation.

BIBLIOGRAPHY

BOOKS

Aggarwal, Raj. Financial Policies for the Multinational Company:
The Management of Foreign Exchange. New York: Praeger, 1976.

Alhashim, Dhia D., and James W. Robertson, eds. Accounting for
Multinational Enterprises. Indianapolis: Bobbs-Merrill, 1978.

Amey, Lloyd R., and Don A. Egginton. Management Accounting:
A Conceptual Approach. London: Longman, 1973.

Angel, Juvenal L., comp. Directory of American Firms Operating
in Foreign Countries. American Encyclopedia of International
Information, vol. 2. 8th ed. New York: Simon & Schuster, 1975.

Anthony, Robert N., and James S. Reece. Management Accounting:
Text and Cases. 5th ed. Homewood, Ill.: Richard D. Irwin,
1975.

Arpan, Jeffrey S. International Intracorporate Pricing: Non-
American Systems and Views. New York: Praeger, 1972.

Benke, Ralph L., Jr., and James Don Edwards. Transfer Pricing:
Techniques and Uses. New York: National Association of Accountants, 1980.

Bierman, Harold, Jr., and Thomas R. Dyckman. Managerial Cost
Accounting. 2nd ed. New York: Macmillan, 1976.

Black, Robert, Stephen Blank, and Elizabeth C. Hanson. Multinationals in Contention: Responses at Governmental and International Levels. New York: Conference Board, 1978.

Bonini, Charles P., Robert K. Jaedicke, and Harvey Wagner, eds.
Management Controls: New Directions in Basic Research. New
York: McGraw-Hill, 1964.

Brooke, Michael Z., and H. Lee Remmers. The Strategy of Multinational Enterprises. New York: American Elsevier, 1970.

Business International Corporation. Setting Intercorporate Pricing. New York: Business International Corporation, 1973.

_____. Solving International Pricing Problems. New York: Business International Corporation, 1965.

Cateora, Philip R., and John M. Hess. International Marketing. 3rd ed. Homewood, Ill.: Richard D. Irwin, 1975.

Chenchall, Robert H., Graeme L. Harrison, and David J. H. Watson. The Organizational Context of Management Accounting. Marshfield, Mass.: Pitman, 1981.

Choi, Frederick D. S., and Gerhard G. Mueller. An Introduction to Multinational Accounting. Englewood Cliffs, N.J.: Prentice-Hall, 1978.

_____, eds. Essentials of Multinational Accounting: An Anthology. New York University Research Project. Ann Arbor, Mich.: University Microfilm International, 1979.

Conference Board. Measuring Profitability of Foreign Operations. New York: Conference Board, 1970.

Cooper, William W., Harold J. Leavitt, and Maynard W. Shelly, II, eds. New Perspectives in Organization Research. New York: John Wiley & Sons, 1969.

Cummings, Larry L., and D. Schwab. Performance in Organizations: Determinants and Appraisal. Glenview, Ill.: Scott, Foresman, 1973.

Duerr, Michael G. Foreign and U.S. Corporate Income and Withholding Tax Rates. Cleveland: Ernst & Ernst, 1978.

_____. The Problems Facing International Management. New York: Conference Board, 1974.

_____. Tax Allocations and International Business: Corporate Experience with Sec. 482 of the Internal Revenue Code. New York: Conference Board, 1972.

Fayerweather, John. International Business Management: A Conceptual Framework. New York: McGraw-Hill, 1969.

Greene, James H., and Michael G. Duerr. Intercompany Transactions in the Multinational Firm. New York: Conference Board, 1970.

Hellmann, Rainer. The Challenge to U.S. Dominance of the International Corporation. Cambridge, Mass.: Dunellen, 1970.

Horngren, Charles T. Cost Accounting: A Managerial Emphasis. 4th ed. Englewood Cliffs, N.J.: Prentice-Hall, 1977.

LaPalombara, Joseph G., and Stephen Blank. Multinational Corporations in Comparative Perspective. New York: Conference Board, 1977.

Lazen, Robert I., and Walter S. Wikstrom. Appraising Managerial Performance: Current Practices and Future Directions. New York: Conference Board, 1977.

Mathewson, G. Frank, and G. David Quirin. Fiscal Transfer Pricing in Multinational Corporations. Ontario Economic Council Research Studies, no. 16. Toronto, Canada: University of Toronto Press, 1979.

Mautz, Robert K. Financial Reporting by Diversified Companies. New York: Financial Executives Research Foundation, 1968.

Miller, Elwood L. Accounting Problems of Multinational Enterprises. Lexington, Mass.: D. C. Heath, 1979.

Moore, Russell M., and George M. Scott, eds. An Introduction to Financial Control and Reporting in Multinational Enterprises. Studies in International Business, no. 1. Austin: The University of Texas, Bureau of Business Research, 1973.

National Association of Accountants. Accounting for Intracompany Transfers. Research Report no. 30. New York: National Association of Accountants, 1956.

_____. Management Accounting Problems in Foreign Operations. Research Report no. 36. New York: National Association of Accountants, 1960.

National Industrial Conference Board. Interdivisional Transfer Pricing. Studies in Business Policy, no. 122. New York: National Industrial Conference Board, 1967.

_____. Managing the International Financial Function. Studies in Business Policy, no. 133. New York: National Industrial Conference Board, 1970.

Nie, Norman H., C. Hadlai Hull, Jean G. Jenkins, Karin Steinbrenner, and Dale H. Bent. Statistical Package for the Social Sciences, 2nd ed. New York: McGraw-Hill, 1975.

Nieckels, Lars. Transfer Pricing in Multinational Firms: A Heuristic Programming Approach and a Case Study. Stockholm, Sweden: Almqvist and Wiksell International, 1976.

Organization for Economic Cooperation and Development. Transfer Pricing and Multinational Enterprises. Paris: OECD, 1979.

Plasschaert, Sylvain R. Transfer Pricing and Multinational Companies: An Overview of Concepts, Mechanisms and Regulation. New York: Praeger, 1979.

Pomper, Claude L. International Investment Planning: An Integrated Approach. New York: North-Holland, 1976.

Robbins, Sidney M., and Robert B. Stobaugh. Money in the Multinational Enterprise: A Study of Financial Policy. New York: Basic Books, 1973.

Robock, Stefan H., Kenneth Simmons, and Jack Zwick. International Business and Multinational Enterprises. Homewood, Ill.: Richard D. Irwin, 1977.

Rolf, Stanley E., and Walter Damm. The Multinational Corporation in the World Economy. New York: Praeger, 1970.

Rook, Angela. Transfer Pricing: A Measurement of Management Performance in Multidivisional Companies. London: British Institute of Management, 1971.

Rugman, Alan M. Multinationals in Canada: Theory, Performance and Economic Impact. Boston: Nijhoff, 1980.

Shillingshaw, Gordon. Managerial Cost Accounting. 4th ed. Homewood, Ill.: Richard D. Irwin, 1977.

Solomons, David. Divisional Performance: Measurement and Control. Homewood, Ill.: Richard D. Irwin, 1965.

Stopford, John M., and Louis T. Wells. Managing the Multinational Enterprise: Organization of the Firm and Ownership of the Subsidiaries. New York: Basic Books, 1972.

Tang, Roger Y. W. Transfer-Pricing Practices in the U.S. and Japan. New York: Praeger, 1979.

Tomkins, Cyril. Financial Planning in Divisionalized Companies. London: Haymarket, 1973.

Vaitsos, Constantine V. Intercompany Income Distribution and Transnational Enterprises. London: Oxford University Press, 1974.

_____. Transfer of Resources and Preservation of Monopoly Rents. Economic Development Report no. 168. Cambridge, Mass.: Harvard University Press, 1970.

Verlage, H. C. Transfer Pricing for Multinational Enterprises. Rotterdam, Netherlands: Rotterdam University Press, 1975.

Weston, J. Fred, and Bart W. Sorge. International Managerial Finance. Homewood, Ill.: Richard D. Irwin, 1972.

Zenoff, David B., and Jack Zwick. International Financial Management. Englewood Cliffs, N.J.: Prentice-Hall, 1969.

ARTICLES

Abdel-Khalik, A. Rashed, and Edward J. Lusk. "Transfer Pricing—A Synthesis." Accounting Review 49 (January 1974):8-23.

Bailey, Andrew D., Jr., and Warren J. Boe. "Goal and Resource Transfers in the Multigoal Organization." Accounting Review 51 (July 1976):559-73.

Barrett, M. Edgar. "Case of the Tangled Transfer Price." Harvard Business Review 55 (May-June 1977):20-22.

Benke, Ralph L., Jr., and James Don Edwards. "Should You Use Transfer Pricing to Create Pseudo-Profit Centers?" Management Accounting 62 (February 1981):36-39, 43.

_____. "Transfer Pricing: Technique and Uses." Management Accounting 61 (June 1980):44-46.

Berkwitt, George J. "The Big Move to Measure Managers." Dun's Review 98 (September 1971):60-62, 64.

Bernhard, Richard H. "Some Problems in Applying Mathematical Programming to Opportunity Cost." Journal of Accounting Research 6 (Spring 1968):143-48.

Bhushan, Rhuwan. "Effects of Inflation and Currency Fluctuation." Management Accounting 56 (July 1974):17-19.

Bierman, Harold, Jr. "Pricing Intracompany Transfers." Accounting Review 34 (July 1959):429-32.

Bond, Eric W. "Optimal Transfer Pricing When Tax Rates Differ." Southern Economic Journal 47 (July 1980):191-200.

Boyd, Robert W. "Transfer Prices and Profitability Measurement." The Controller 29 (February 1961):88-89.

Boyer, Jean P. "Intercompany Pricing's Effect on R.O.I. Analysis." Financial Executive 32 (December 1964):20-26.

Brantner, Paul F. "Taxation and the Multinational Firm." Management Accounting 55 (October 1973):11-16, 26.

Broom, H. N. "A Method of Accounting for Interdepartmental Profits." Accounting Review 23 (October 1948):417-20.

Butler, Robert E. "The Planning Process: Vital Elements That Are Often Overlooked." Price Waterhouse Review 23 (1978):56-64.

Camman, Eric A. "Interdepartmental Profits." Journal of Accountancy 48 (July 1929):37-44.

Chasteen, Lanny G. "Shadow Prices: A Graphical Approach." Management Accounting 54 (September 1972):27-29.

Choudhury, Nandan. "Transfer Pricing Practices: Room for Debate." Accountancy 90 (August 1979):105-6.

Cook, Paul W., Jr. "Decentralization and the Transfer-Price Problem." Journal of Business 28 (April 1955):87-94.

_____. "New Technique for Intracompany Pricing." Harvard Business Review 35 (July-August 1957):74-81.

Cowen, Scott S., Lawrence C. Phillips, and Linda Stillabower. "Multinational Transfer Pricing." Management Accounting 60 (January 1979):17-22.

Cyert, Richard M., William R. Dill, and James G. March. "The Role of Expectations in Business Decision-Making." Administrative Science Quarterly 3 (December 1958):307-40.

Dagher, Samir P. "What's the Price When a Company Buys from Itself?" Administrative Management 37 (May 1977):32-33.

Dascher, Paul E. "Transfer Pricing—Some Behavioral Observations." Managerial Planning 21 (November-December 1972): 17-21.

Dean, Joel. "Decentralization and Intracompany Pricing." Harvard Business Review 33 (July-August 1955):65-74.

_____. "Profit Performance Measurement of Division Managers." The Controller 25 (September 1957):423-24, 426, 449.

Dearden, John. "Appraising Profit-Center Managers." Harvard Business Review 46 (May-June 1968):80-87.

_____. "The Case Against ROI Control." Harvard Business Review 47 (May-June 1969):124-35.

_____. "The Case of the Disputing Divisions: How Should Decentralized Organizations Handle the Interdivisional Pricing Problem?" Harvard Business Review 42 (May-June 1964):158-59.

_____. "Interdivisional Pricing." Harvard Business Review 38 (January-February 1960):117-25.

_____. "Limits on Decentralized Profit Responsibility." Harvard Business Review 40 (July-August 1962):81-89.

_____. "Mirage of Profit Decentralization." Harvard Business Review 40 (November-December 1962):140-43.

_____. "Problems in Decentralized Financial Control." Harvard Business Review 39 (May-June 1961):72-84.

_____. "Problems in Decentralized Profit Responsibility." Harvard Business Review 38 (May-June 1960):79-86.

Demski, Joel S., and Gerald A. Feltham. "Economic Incentives in Budgetary Control Systems." Accounting Review 53 (April 1978): 336-59.

Dietemann, Gerard J. "Evaluating Multinational Performance under FASB No. 8." Management Accounting 61 (May 1980):49-55.

Dittman, David A. "Transfer Pricing and Decentralization." Management Accounting 54 (November 1972):47-50.

Dopuch, Nicholas, and David F. Drake. "Accounting Implications of a Mathematical Programming Approach to the Transfer-Price Problem." Journal of Accounting Research 2 (Spring 1964):10-24.

Drebin, Allen R. "A Proposal for Dual Pricing of Intracompany Transfers." NAA Bulletin 40 (February 1959):51-55.

Earnest, Kenneth R. "Applying Motivational Theory in Management Accounting." Management Accounting 61 (December 1979):41-44.

Edwards, James Don, and Roger A. Roemmich. "Transfer Pricing: The Wrong Tool for Performance Evaluation." Cost and Management 50 (January-February 1976):35-37.

Emmanuel, Clive. "Transfer Pricing: A Diagnosis and Possible Solution to Dysfunctional Decision Making in the Divisionalized Company." Management International Review 17 (1977):45-59.

Fantl, Irving L. "Transfer Pricing—Tread Carefully." CPA Journal 44 (December 1974):42-46.

Ferrara, William L. "Accounting for Performance Evaluation and Decision Making." Management Accounting 58 (December 1976): 13-19.

Finney, Frederick D. "Pricing Interdivisional Transfers." Management Accounting 48 (November 1966):10-18.

Finnie, John. "Transfer-Pricing Practices." Management Accounting 56 (December 1978):494-97.

Fremgen, James M. "Measuring the Profit of Part of a Firm." Management Accounting 47 (January 1966):26-29.

_____. "Transfer Pricing and Management Goals." Management Accounting 52 (December 1970):25-31.

Gaedala, Ralph M., and Dennis H. Tootelian. "The Fortune 500 List—An Endangered Species for Academic Research." Journal of Business Research 4 (August 1976):283-88.

Garda, J. A. "The Measurement of Financial Data in Evaluating Overseas Managerial Efficiency." International Journal of Accounting 12 (Fall 1976):13-17.

Gee, Kenneth P. "A Cash-Flow Measure of Divisional Performance." The Accountant's Magazine 84 (January 1980):17-20.

Goetz, Billy E. "Transfer Prices. An Exercise in Relevancy and Goal Congruence." Accounting Review 42 (July 1967):435-40.

Gordon, Myron J. "A Method of Pricing for a Socialist Economy." Accounting Review 45 (July 1970):427-43.

Gould, John R. "Internal Pricing in Firms When There Are Costs of Using an Outside Market." Journal of Business 37 (January 1964):61-67.

Greene, James. "Intercorporate Pricing across National Frontiers." Conference Board Record 6 (October 1969):43-48.

Greer, Howard. "Divisional Profit Calculation—Notes on the Transfer-Pricing Problem." NAA Bulletin 43 (July 1962):5-12.

Haidinger, Timothy P. "Negotiate for Profits." Management Accounting 52 (December 1970):23-24, 52.

Hass, Jerome E. "Transfer Pricing in a Decentralized Firm." Management Science 14 (February 1968):B310-33.

Henderson, Bruce D., and John Dearden. "New System for Divisional Control." Harvard Business Review 44 (September-October 1966):144-60.

Hirshleifer, Jack. "Economics of the Divisionalized Firm." Journal of Business 30 (April 1957):96-108.

_____. "Internal Pricing and Decentralized Decisions." In Management Controls: New Directions in Basic Research, edited by Charles A. Bonini, Robert Jaedicke, and Harvey Wagner. New York: McGraw-Hill, 1964.

_____. "On the Economics of Transfer Pricing." Journal of Business 29 (July 1956):172-84.

Holstrum, Gary L., and Eugene H. Sauls. "The Opportunity Cost Transfer Price." Management Accounting 54 (May 1973):29-33.

Holzman, Robert S. "IRS Amplifies the Rules for Intercompany Transactions." Management Review 57 (July 1968):37-41.

Hopwood, Anthony G. "An Empirical Study of the Role of Accounting Data in Performance Evaluation." Journal of Accounting Research Supplement 10 (1972):156-93.

Horst, Thomas. "The Theory of the Multinational Firm: Optimal Behavior under Different Tariff and Tax Rates." Journal of Political Economy 79 (September-October 1971):1059-72.

Itami, Hiroyuki. "Evaluating Measures and Goal Congruence under Uncertainty." Journal of Accounting Research 13 (Spring 1975): 73-96.

Kanodia, Chandra. "Risk Sharing and Transfer-Price Systems under Uncertainty." Journal of Accounting Research 17 (Spring 1979):74-98.

Keegan, Warren J. "Multinational Pricing: How Far Is Arm's-Length?" Columbia Journal of World Business 4 (May-June 1969):57-66.

Kerin, Rodger A., and Michael G. Harvey. "Methodological Considerations in Corporate Mail Surveys: A Research Note." Journal of Business Research 4 (August 1976):277-81.

Kim, Seung L., and Stephen W. Miller. "Constituents of the International Transfer-Pricing Decision." Columbia Journal of World Business 14 (Spring 1979):69-77.

Lambert, David R. "Transfer Pricing and Interdivisional Conflict." California Management Review 21 (Summer 1979):70-75.

Lamp, Walter. "The Multinational Whipping Boy." Financial Executive 44 (December 1976):44-46.

Larson, Raymond L. "Decentralization in Real Life." Management Accounting 55 (March 1974):28-32.

Lemke, Kenneth W. "In Defense of the 'Profit Center' Concept." Abacus 6 (December 1970):182–88.

Lessard, Donald R., and Peter Lorange. "Currency Changes and Management Control: Resolving the Centralization/Decentralization Dilemma." Accounting Review 52 (July 1977):628–37.

Levinson, Harry. "Appraisal of What Performance." Harvard Business Review 54 (July–August 1976):30–32.

Li, David H. "Interdivisional Transfer Planning." Management Accounting 46 (June 1965):51–54.

Littrell, Earl K. "Taking a Dim View of Profits." Management Accounting 61 (March 1980):60.

MacGregor, Douglas. "An Uneasy Look at Performance Appraisal." Harvard Business Review 35 (May–June 1957):89–94.

McLanin, Robert. "Transfer Pricing Can Contribute to Divisional Profit Performance." NAA Bulletin 44 (August 1963):29–32.

Madison, Roland L. "Responsibility Accounting and Transfer Pricing: Approach with Caution." Management Accounting 60 (January 1979):25–29.

Malmstrom, Duane. "Accommodating Exchange–Rate Fluctuations in Intercompany Pricing and Invoicing." Management Accounting 59 (September 1977):24–28.

Mauriel, John J. "Evaluation and Control of Overseas Operations." Management Accounting 50 (May 1969):35–39, 52.

Mauriel, John J., and Robert N. Anthony. "Misevaluation of Investment Center Performance." Harvard Business Review 44 (March–April 1966):98–105.

Menge, John A. "The Backward Art of Interdivisional Transfer Pricing." Journal of Industrial Economics 9 (July 1961):215–32.

Metcalf, Mike. "Related Party Transactions—Why a Standard Is Needed." Accountancy 90 (May 1979):99–100.

Meyer, Herbert H., Emanuel Kay, and John R. P. French, Jr. "Split Roles in Performance Appraisal." Harvard Business Review 43 (January–February 1965):123–29.

Milburn, J. Alex. "International Transfer Transactions: What Price?" CA Magazine 109 (December 1976):22-27.

Murphy, Robert W. "Corporate Divisions vs. Subsidiaries." Harvard Business Review 34 (November-December 1956):83-92.

Nagy, Richard J. "Transfer-Price Accounting for Multinational Corporations." Management Accounting 59 (January 1978):34-38.

Onsi, Mohamed. "A Transfer-Pricing System Based on Opportunity Cost." Accounting Review 45 (July 1970):535-43.

_____. "Transfer-Pricing System Based on Opportunity Cost: A Reply." Accounting Review 49 (January 1974):129-31.

Parker, Lee D. "Divisional Performance Measurement: Beyond an Exclusive Profit Test." Accounting and Business Research 9 (Autumn 1979):309-19.

_____. "Management Accounting and the Corporate Environment." Management Accounting 59 (February 1978):15-20, 26.

Petty, J. W., II, and Ernest W. Walker. "Optimal Transfer Pricing for the Multinational Firm." Financial Management 1 (Winter 1972):74-84.

Piper, A. G. "Internal Trading." Accountancy 80 (October 1969): 733-36.

Rao, K. R. M., and James C. Baker. "Transfer-of-Funds Model for International Corporations." Managerial Planning 27 (January-February 1979):32-38.

Reece, James S., and William R. Cool. "Measuring Investment Center Performance." Harvard Business Review 56 (May-June 1978):28-30.

Reider, George A. "Performance Review—A Mixed Bag." Harvard Business Review 51 (July-August 1973):61-67.

Ridgway, Valentine F. "Dysfunctional Consequences of Performance Measurements." Administrative Science Quarterly 1 (September 1956):240-47.

Robbins, Sidney M., and Robert B. Stobaugh. "The Bent Measuring Stick for Foreign Subsidiaries." Harvard Business Review 51 (September–October 1973):80–88.

Ronen, Joshua, and G. McKinney. "Transfer Pricing for Divisional Autonomy." Journal of Accounting Research 8 (Spring 1970): 99–112.

Rutenberg, David P. "Maneuvering Liquid Assets in a Multinational Company: Formulation and Deterministic Solution Procedures." Management Science 16 (June 1970):B671–B683.

Samuels, J. M. "Opportunity Costing: An Application of Mathematical Programming." Journal of Accounting Research 3 (Autumn 1965):182–91.

Schwab, Richard J. "A Contribution Approach to Transfer Pricing." Management Accounting 56 (February 1975):46–48.

Seghers, Paul D. "How to Set and Defend Intercompany Prices Under Section 482 Regulations." Taxes 47 (October 1969):606–22.

Sharav, Itzhak. "Transfer Pricing—Diversity of Goals and Practices." Journal of Accountancy 137 (April 1974):56–62.

Shaub, H. James. "Transfer Pricing in a Decentralized Organization." Management Accounting 59 (April 1978):33–36, 42.

Shillinglaw, Gordon. "Guides to Internal Profit Measurement." Harvard Business Review 35 (March–April 1957):82–94.

_____. "Problems in Divisional Profit Measurement." NAA Bulletin 42 (March 1961):33–43.

_____. "Toward a Theory of Divisional Income Measurement." Accounting Review 37 (April 1962):208–16.

Shulman, James S. "Transfer Pricing in the Multinational Firm." European Business, January 1969, pp. 46–54.

_____. "When the Price is Wrong—By Design." Columbia Journal of World Business 2 (May–June 1967):69–76.

Solomons, David. "Intra Corporate Conflict in International Business." In Topics in Accounting and Planning, edited by Richard Mattessich. Vancouver, Canada: University of British Columbia, 1972.

Stanley, Curtis H. "Cost-Basis Valuations in Transactions between Entities." Accounting Review 39 (July 1964):639-47.

Stewart, James C. "Multinational Companies and Transfer Pricing." Journal of Business, Finance and Accounting 4 (Autumn 1977): 353-71.

Stitt, Hubert J., and John Connor. "International Intercompany Pricing." Canadian Tax Journal 10 (March-April 1962):85-92.

Stone, Willard E. "Intercompany Pricing." Accounting Review 31 (October 1956):625-27.

_____. "Legal Implications of Intracompany Pricing." Accounting Review 39 (January 1964):38-42.

_____. "Tax Considerations in Intracompany Pricing." Accounting Review 35 (January 1960):45-58.

Tang, Roger Y. W. "Canadian Transfer-Pricing Practices." CA Magazine 113 (March 1980):32-38.

Tang, Roger Y. W., C. K. Walter, and Robert H. Raymond. "Transfer Pricing: Japanese Versus American Style." Management Accounting 60 (January 1979):12-16.

Thomas, Arthur L. "Transfer Prices in the Multinational Firm: When Will They Be Arbitrary?" Abacus 7 (June 1971):40-53.

Troxel, Richard B. "On Transfer Pricing." CPA Journal 43 (October 1973):895-97.

Tse, Paul S. "Evaluating Performance in Multinationals." Management Accounting 60 (June 1979):21-25.

Vancil, Richard F. "What Kind of Management Control Do You Need?" Harvard Business Review 51 (March-April 1973):75-86.

Vendig, Richard E. "A Three-Part Transfer Price." Management Accounting 55 (September 1973):33-36.

Villers, Raymond. "Control and Freedom in a Decentralized Company." Harvard Business Review 32 (March–April 1954):89–96.

Walter, John T. "The Eli Lilly Decision." Taxes 45 (September 1967):622–24.

Watson, David J. H., and John V. Baumler. "Transfer Pricing: A Behavioral Context." Accounting Review 50 (July 1975):466–74.

Weinwurm, Ernest H. "Measuring Executive Performance." In Management Science: Models and Techniques, edited by C. West Churchman and Michel Verhulst. Oxford, England: Pergamon, 1960.

Wells, M. C. "Profit Centers, Transfer Prices, and Mysticism." Abacus 4 (December 1968):174–81.

_____. "Transfer Prices and Profit Centers?" No." Abacus 7 (June 1971):54–57.

Wilkinson, Joseph W. "The Meanings of Measurements." Management Accounting 57 (July 1975):49–57.

Wodjak, Joseph. "An Introduction to the External Aspects of Transfer Pricing." New York CPA 38 (May 1968):341–52.

DISSERTATIONS

Ackelsberg, M. Robert. "Transfer Pricing: Its Behavioral Consequences." Ph.D. dissertation, City University of New York, 1977.

Bisat, Talal A. "An Evaluation of International Intercompany Transactions." Ph.D. dissertation, American University, 1967.

Gerardi, Geraldine Ann. "Transfer Pricing and Profit Shifting: An Empirical Analysis." Ph.D. dissertation, American University, 1976.

Jenson, Oscar William. "Transfer Pricing and Tax Policy for the Multinational Corporation." Ph.D. dissertation, University of Connecticut, 1976.

Milburn, J. Alex. "International Transfer Pricing in a Financial Accounting Context." Ph. D. dissertation, University of Illinois, 1977.

Okpechi, Simeon O. "Interdivisional Transfer Pricing: A Conflict Resolution Approach." Ph. D. dissertation, Ohio State University, 1976.

Petty, John W. "An Optimal Transfer-Pricing System for the Multinational Firm: A Linear Programming Approach." Ph. D. dissertation, University of Texas, 1971.

Shulman, James S. "Transfer Pricing in Multinational Business." D. B. A. dissertation, Harvard University, 1966.

Stone, Willard E. "Management Practices with Respect to Internal Transfer Pricing in Large Manufacturing Companies." Ph. D. dissertation, University of Pennsylvania, 1957.

Tang, Roger Y. W. "An Empirical Investigation of the Transfer-Pricing Practices of Large Industrial Corporations in the United States and Japan." Ph. D. dissertation, University of Nebraska, 1977.

INDEX

accountability, 33

actual values versus estimated, 52

administration versus policy formulation, 10

American Encyclopedia of International Information (Vol. 2: Directory of American Firms Operating in Foreign Countries), 45

antitrust aspects of transfer pricing, 38

artificial distribution of profit, 144

artificial transfer prices, 125

associative relationships, 21, 53, 139; versus causative relationships, 8, 54

autonomy policy, 2, 6, 26-34, 98-104, 140, 143; and performance-evaluation policy, 119-21, 144; and transfer-pricing policy, 121-25, 144-45

average (see mean)

behavioral literature, 38

Boston Consulting Group matrix, 13

budgets and goals, 32

buying subsidiary, 11

cash cow, 13

causal relationships, 21, 52, 139; versus associative relationships, 8, 54

centers, 27, 69

centralization versus decentralization, 34, 100, 103

Columbia Journal of World Business, 48

complements versus substitutes, 56, 59

concentration of resources, 13

consistency in goals, 32

control variables, 8 (see also instrument variables)

controlled experiment, 52

corporate characteristics, 2-3

corporate control policy, 7

corporate policy, 27; constraints on

subsidiary profits, 9-10

correlation, 53-56

cost center, 27, 34, 38, 69

cost reduction, 121

cross-tabulation, 135

currency value fluctuations, 14, 104

current business orientation, 69

customs duty payments, 36

decentralization (see autonomy)

decentralization versus centralization, 100, 103

decision making under uncertainty, 7-8

decreasing cost (see economies of scale)

degrees of freedom, 61-62, 63

dependent variables, 52

descriptive statistics, 21, 51

deviations, 52

distribution of profit among subsidiaries, 10-11

dollar measures versus local currency, 104

dual pricing, 37

Dun and Bradstreet's Million Dollar Directory, 45

economies of scale, 13

environmental factors or variables, 6, 7-8, 9, 15-17, 27, 29, 32, 74 (see also key exogenous variables)

endogenous factors, 21

environmental variability (ENVA), 63, 108

equitable transfer price, 11

errors, 52

estimated versus actual values, 52

evaluation period, 32

exchange rates, 32, 36 (see also currency value fluctuations)

exogenous factors or variables, 7-8, 21, 64 (see also key exogenous factors)

expense center, 27

external dealing instruments, 100

Financial Executives Research Council, 48
foreign sales ratio, 61
foreign subsidiary ratio, 61
Fortune 500, 45
frequency distributions, 68

given characteristics, 6
goal congruence, 33
goals and budgets, 32
goals, multiplicity of, 10

headquarters unit, 6
heavy weighting versus light weighting, 117
high-keyed versus low-keyed respondents, 108, 109, 111
high transfer price, 11

incremental cost transfer pricing, 37
independent variables, 52 (see also exogenous factors or variables)
inefficiency of managers, 9
instrumental transfer prices, 35, 38-39, 64, 100, 103, 116-17, 121-25, 126, 128, 130, 135, 144
instrument variables, 7, 27, 98-103
internal dealing instruments, 100
intracorporate conflict, 38
investment center, 27, 69

key exogenous variables, 56, 59, 61-63, 139; effect on autonomy policy, 100-103, 140; effect on performance-evaluation policy, 106, 108, 143; effect on transfer-pricing policy, 117, 119, 143
least squares, 52
light weighting versus heavy weighting, 117
linear relationship, 52
local currency versus dollar measures, 104
long-run versus short-run profit orientation, 10, 62-63, 100-1
long-term business instruments, 100
long-term performance versus short-term performance, 29
lost contribution margin, 38
low-keyed versus high-keyed respondents, 108, 109

low transfer prices, 11, 12-13, 35, 123, 125, 128-29, 144

manager evaluation versus subsidiary evaluation, 104
marginal cost transfer pricing, 36, 37
market-oriented transfer prices, 11-12, 35, 121-22, 126, 144
mathematical programming transfer prices, 37
maximization of parent company welfare, 8; of subsidiary manager benefits, 7-8
mean, 16, 51
missing observations, 50
multicollinearity, 66, 68
multiple choice judgments, 17, 50
multiple criteria in performance evaluation, 31-32
multiple regression, 52-53

National Industrial Conference Board, 49
natural distribution of profit, 11
normal distribution, 55, 145
null hypothesis, 54-55
number of countries, 66
number of subsidiaries, 66

objective versus subjective standards, 104, 106
observable success criteria, 27
organizations, 26

parent unit, 6
partial correlation, 52-53, 139; versus simple correlation, 53-54
"Pearson product moment," correlation coefficient, 53
perception of environment, 63
performance-evaluation policy, 7, 26-34, 104-9; and autonomy policy, 119-21, 144; and transfer-pricing policy, 2, 9-14, 36, 39, 125-35, 144-45
performance evaluations of managers versus subsidiaries, 9, 104
policy formulation versus administration, 10

ABOUT THE AUTHOR

PENELOPE J. YUNKER was born in 1945 in Derby, England, came to the United States in 1966, and was naturalized as a U.S. citizen in 1976. After taking a Bachelor of Business Administration (1975) and an M.A. in Accounting (1976) from Western Illinois University, she worked for two years as an Instructor in Accountancy at W.I.U. before enrolling in the Ph.D. program at St. Louis University in the summer of 1978.

While at S.L.U., Ms. Yunker majored in Accounting and minored in International Business. Under the direction of S.L.U.'s specialist in accounting for multinationals, Elwood L. Miller, she investigated the problem of transfer pricing and performance evaluation and carried out a survey of multinational corporations during the winter of 1980-81. Her dissertation analyzing the survey results was completed at St. Louis University in December 1981.

Currently an Assistant Professor of Accountancy at Western Illinois University, she resides in Macomb, Illinois, with her husband James, a Professor of Economics at W.I.U. In addition to her work on transfer pricing and performance evaluation, she has published in the area of cost-volume-profit analysis under uncertainty, and has further projects underway relating to financial accounting in multinational corporations.